Young Readers Edition

THE MAMMALS

Adapted from a text by Richard Carrington

with additions by the Editors of TIME-LIFE BOOKS

TIME INCORPORATED, NEW YORK

ON THE COVER: The red fox, a member of the wild dog family, is found in most of the Northern Hemisphere. Accused of being a chicken thief, he subsists mostly on mice, insects, grass and wild fruits.

TIME
LIFE
BOOKS
®

LIFE WORLD LIBRARY

LIFE NATURE LIBRARY

TIME READING PROGRAM

THE LIFE HISTORY OF THE UNITED STATES

LIFE SCIENCE LIBRARY

GREAT AGES OF MAN

TIME-LIFE LIBRARY OF ART

TIME-LIFE LIBRARY OF AMERICA

FOODS OF THE WORLD

THIS FABULOUS CENTURY

LIFE LIBRARY OF PHOTOGRAPHY

Contents

Introduction

Mankind's rise through evolution to a position of dominance among the earth's creatures has been closely linked to the history of the whole class of mammals—of which man himself is a member. Even today man still makes use of other mammals as a source of food and drink, clothing and cover, power and transportation, chemicals and companionship. Despite his dependence on mammals, man has usually confined his interest to those few dozen species that are of direct use or harm to him. The rest he has tended to ignore.

Yet man is physically inferior to other mammals in many ways. It is only in the past century that he has been able to cross land, water or air faster than a cheetah, porpoise or bat. In our own time, even with the aid of machines, man's hearing, for example, remains much less acute than the bat's, and atomic submarines cannot dive as deep as the sperm whale.

Obviously then, man still has much to learn from his fellow mammals. Because he is one of their "classmates," he faces many of the same problems. Food gathering, housing, reproduction and social behavior are all matters of great importance to man, just as they are to every member of the mammalian class. There are many ways to solve these problems, and in this book, in words and pictures, are presented some of the methods that many of the world's mammals have employed to meet and conquer the challenges that life presents.

THE EDITORS OF TIME-LIFE BOOKS

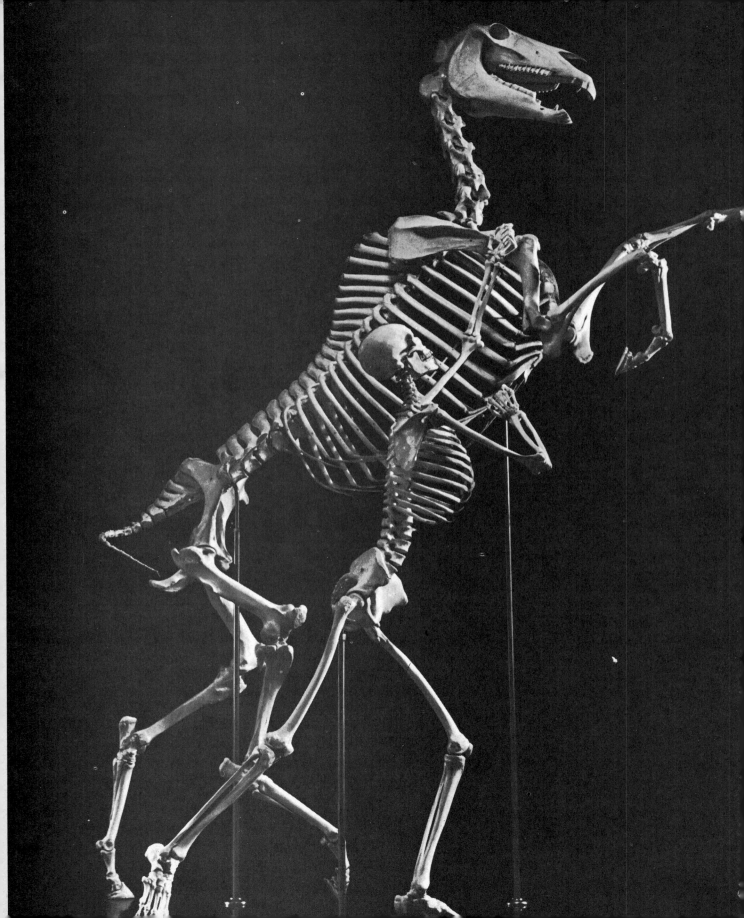

1
The Amazing, Varied World of Mammals

THE SKELETONS of a horse and a man reveal one of the characteristics they have in common: backbones. Other animals that are not mammals—the fish, amphibians, reptiles and birds—also have backbones. Some features that distinguish mammals— milk glands and hair—appear only on their flesh.

When the word animal is mentioned, the image of a dog, cat, cow, lion or tiger springs to mind. Indeed, all *are* animals; but they are something else besides—a special kind of animal called a mammal. In everyday speech animal and mammal are frequently used as if they meant the same thing. This is only a half truth. The term animal includes birds, snakes, frogs, flies, spiders, fish—even the worm that baits the hook that catches the fish. But none of these is a mammal.

What, then, are mammals? How do they differ from all other creatures? And what are the factors that unite into one immense group creatures as different as a 130-ton blue whale and a shrew weighing one tenth of an ounce, a massive elephant and a fluttering bat, a ponderous hippopotamus and a fleet-footed jaguar?

Some features of mammals also are found in other creatures. All mammals have backbones. The skeletons of two very different mammals, man and the horse (*opposite*), display this trait. But birds, fishes, reptiles and amphibians have backbones too. It is true, also, that mammals breathe air, but so do

Nursing Methods That Differ

Three kinds of mammals show the different ways they feed their young. The platypus, a monotreme, hatches its young from eggs and feeds them from pores on its abdomen. The opossum, a marsupial, gives birth to living but incompletely developed babies; for many weeks they live inside a pouch, firmly attached to their mother's nipples. The young of the giraffe, a placental mammal, are active from birth and nurse at intervals.

MONOTREME: PLATYPUS

PLACENTAL: GIRAFFE

MARSUPIAL: OPOSSUM

birds, reptiles, most insects and amphibians. Almost every mammal gives birth to live young—but many reptiles and fish do this as well.

There are, in addition, some specialized features that are possessed only by mammals and that single out this group from all other animals. Among these are the ability to produce milk from special glands, which is fed to the young (*opposite*), and the presence of true hair on the animal at some stage of its growth. It is true that some pigeons and insects produce fluids that for convenience are sometimes called milk. But this so-called "milk" is as different from the milk of mammals as a strawberry malted is from cough medicine.

It is also true that some insects—and, indeed, some plants—have growths generally referred to as hair, but these are totally different in structure and function from mammalian hair. There are, of course, mammals such as whales and porpoises that are almost totally hairless when fully grown. But all mammals, at some stage of their lives, have hair.

Mammals also have a number of other internal characteristics that set them apart. The number of bones that make up the skull, for example, is fewer in mammals than in other creatures with backbones. Mammalian teeth differ from the teeth of other animals in their variety. Most mammals have several different kinds of teeth; some are for chewing, others for stabbing, gnaw-ing, grinding or grabbing the food they eat.

All mammals are warm-blooded. This means that they are able to keep their body temperatures at a constant level despite drastic changes in air temperature. (Warm-bloodedness is hardly unique to mammals; birds, too, have it, and, under certain conditions, so do some reptiles.) The arctic fox, for example, maintains its normal body temperature even when the winter thermometer falls to −112° F., and when the summer sun warms the northern air.

Not all mammals, of course, can withstand so extreme a range of temperature, but all mammals have the ability in greater or lesser degree. Some mammals are exceptions to this rule; their temperatures often fall very close to freezing. This is true of those, such as woodchucks and ground squirrels, that go into a deep "sleep" during the winter—called hibernation.

To keep from freezing in winter is only half the mammal's battle; it must also keep from burning up in summer. One way in which the body cools itself is by losing water, either through sweating or panting.

Maintaining a high body temperature requires mammals to eat more frequently and with more regularity than do such cold-blooded creatures as reptiles. Food is fuel for mammals, and food burned up in the form of energy must be replaced constantly. In other words, just as a furnace must be repeatedly stoked with coal or oil, a mammal must be repeatedly replenished with food.

echidna

platypus

MONOTREMATA

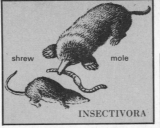

shrew

mole

INSECTIVORA

colugo

DERMOPTERA

bat

CHIROPTERA

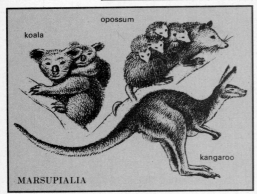

koala

opossum

kangaroo

MARSUPIALIA

man

tree shrew

chimpanzee

monkey

lemur

PRIMATES

The insulating ability of hair and the cooling ability of sweat glands combine to give mammals an enormous advantage: they can remain active through a wide range of climatic conditions. Reptiles, lacking these advantages, quickly die from high heat and become listless in cold. On the other hand, since reptiles are less dependent on continual nourishment than mammals, they need not be as active, for they are not required to find food as often or as regularly.

Mammals have one other important advantage over other creatures: they are more intelligent. The tricks that dogs, sea lions, dolphins and apes can learn are only one small indication of mammalian intelligence. Wolves help other wolves and killer whales help each other by hunting in packs. Monkeys and apes have shown a particularly high order of intelligence; chimpanzees, a kind of ape, even show some ability to think up solutions to problems they have never

CARNIVORA

bear

otter

wolf

sea lion

lion

PROBOSCID

elephant

TUBULIDENTATA

aardvark

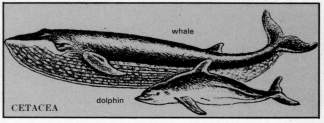

sloth

anteater

armadillo

ENTATA

pangolin

PHOLIDOTA

LAGOMORPHA

jack rabbit

pika

squirrel

beaver

capybara

rat

porcupine

RODENTIA

whale

CETACEA

dolphin

Mammals: A Multifaceted Kingdom

All the 4,287 known species, or particular types, of living
mammals fall into one or another of the 18 orders—groups of closely
related animals—shown here. The scientific name of each order,
such as Monotremata or Insectivora, is shown in large type, while
the common names of animals within an order are printed in
small type. All these animals are members of the mammal "family"
because they share traits found only in mammals. These traits
include: milk glands to feed their young, the possession of hair at
some time during the animal's development, similarities in bone
structures and blood vessels, and more highly developed brains.

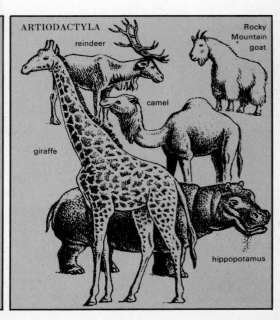

RACOIDEA

hyrax

SIRENIA

manatee

PERISSODACTYLA

horse

rhinoceros

tapir

ARTIODACTYLA

reindeer

Rocky
Mountain
goat

camel

giraffe

hippopotamus

Air Conditioning for Mammals

The scales of reptiles and the skin of mammals are signs of different lines of evolution: reptiles are cold-blooded and mammals warm-blooded. This means a reptile's temperature changes with the air around it; in hot weather scales keep the animal from drying out, but also keep it hot because it cannot cool off by perspiring. Mammals, however, keep their temperature constant; in cold weather fur holds heat in. In hot weather they lose moisture to keep cool.

REPTILE: CROCODILE

before faced. They quickly learn that the best way to get to a bunch of bananas hanging out of reach is to knock it down with a long stick. Some investigators have found that chimpanzees can learn to stack up boxes and climb on them to reach food. But even the brightest chimpanzee cannot compare with the most intelligent mammal of all: man.

The advantages that mammals possess have made them dominant animals in the world. So adept are mammals at adjusting to a variety of conditions of all kinds that they prosper in almost every climate, on land, in the sea and even, as in the case of bats, in the air.

Despite their dominant position, mammals are very few in kind, compared with some other animal groups. There are more than three quarters of a million different varieties of insects and thousands of new ones are being identified every year. In contrast, mammals total a mere 4,300 species.

Each one of these species is in its own way unique. Those species that are closely related are grouped together by zoologists

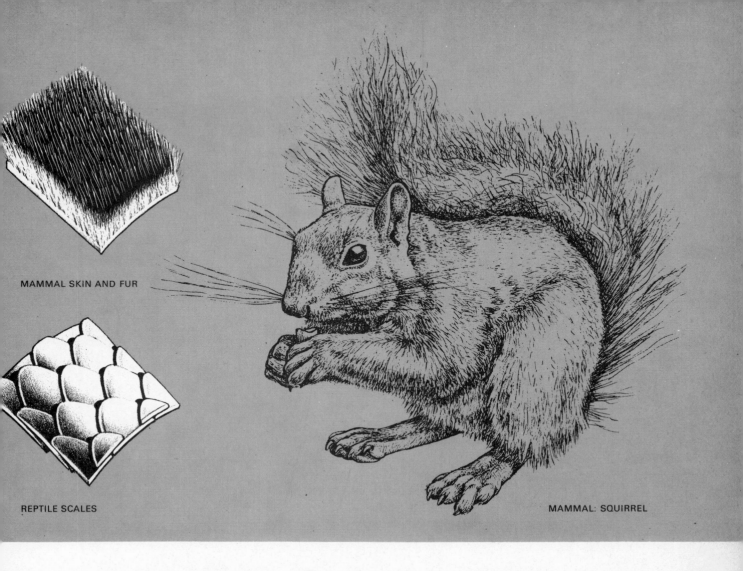

MAMMAL SKIN AND FUR

REPTILE SCALES

MAMMAL: SQUIRREL

into categories called genera. There are about 1,044 genera, grouped into some 125 families; the families are further grouped into 18 different orders of mammals. Some members of each order are shown on pages 10 and 11.

All mammals are descended from reptiles, and the most primitive order of mammals, the monotremes, retains some reptilian characteristics. These strange beasts, found only in Australasia, include only five species—the duck-billed platypus and four kinds of spiny anteaters. Monotremes are unique among living mammals because they lay eggs, like some reptiles, instead of bearing live young. Monotremes also differ from all other mammals in the way in which their young obtain milk. The other mammals have nipples on which the young suck to get their nourishment. But monotremes have no nipples; instead milk oozes from pores in the abdomen, and the young lap the fluid up from the mother's fur (*page 8*). Yet monotremes do produce milk, they do have hair and they are warm-blooded, and therefore they must be counted as mammals.

Another distinctive order is the marsupi-

13

als, found in Australasia and the Americas. Unlike monotremes, marsupials give birth to living babies, but the infants are not fully developed. Some marsupial females have pouches on their abdomens, inside which the young remain to feed on their mother's milk until they are mature enough to live independently. Other marsupials lack pouches, and the young hang on to the mother as she moves about.

Kangaroos are the most familiar marsupials. There are many species, varying in size from the foot-high wallaby and the rat kangaroo to the red kangaroo, taller than most men when it stands on its hind legs.

One strange marsupial is the flying phalanger (*page 18*), which might be mistaken for a twin of the flying squirrel. Actually the two mammals are not even close relatives, but because they lead similar lives they have developed similar body shapes.

It is quite a common occurrence to find unrelated animals that look alike. Zoologists call this kind of evolutionary development convergence. Another common form of evolutionary change is adaptive radiation. Radiation produces radically different outward appearances in closely related species. It occurs when near relatives adapt to entirely different ways of life, resulting in very different body shapes. For example, the bear and the sea lion have radiated from a common ancestor.

Egg-laying monotremes, as well as marsupials with their underdeveloped babies, are

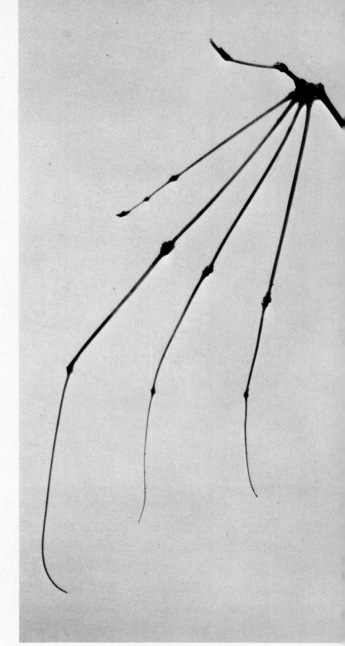

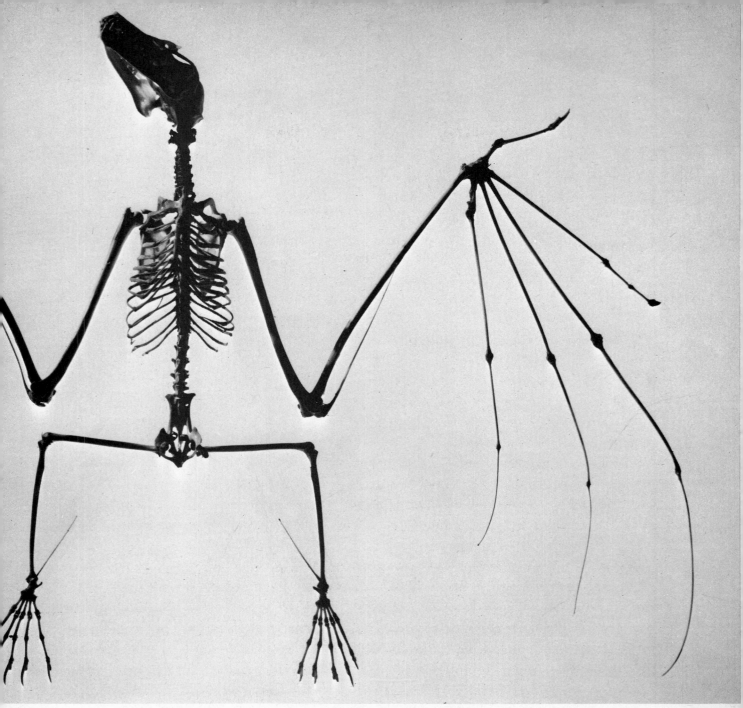

The Bat's Frail Frame

Thin and delicate, the skeleton of a fruit bat has much the same basic bone structure shared by all other mammals, including the horse and man (*page 6*). But the bat is adapted for flight. Its elongated fingers are the supporting parts of its wings, which are connected to its body and hind legs.

15

The Better to Run

Hoofed animals, the ungulates, once had five toes on each foot, but some toes have disappeared through evolution. The horse and the rhinoceros, for example, now have an odd number of toes. The hoof of a horse is actually the nail of its middle toe. Others, such as deer and pigs, have hoofs at the end of an even number of toes. However, not all ungulates have distinct hoofs: the camel and the hippopotamus still have distinct toes.

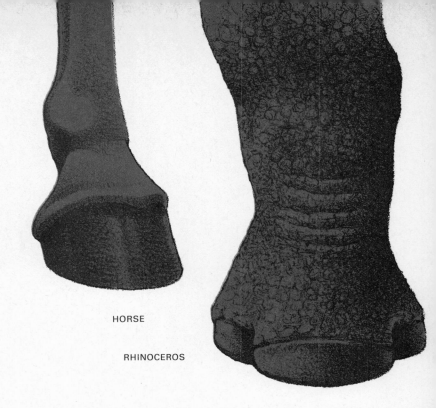

HORSE

RHINOCEROS

oddities of the mammalian world. All the remaining 16 orders of mammals form a grouping that zoologists call placentals. This word refers to an organ—the placenta—inside the mother's body through which an unborn baby draws its food. The great advantage of this system is that most species of placental infants are wholly protected within their mother for a far longer time than either the monotremes or the marsupials. And some placental infants are so well developed at birth they can walk and run within a few hours.

A placental order with very few species is the Dermoptera (literally, skin-wings), which is comprised only of the colugos, or flying lemurs. Like the flying squirrels and flying phalangers, colugos live in treetops and glide from tree to tree on a thin membrane of skin stretching out from the sides of their bodies.

The Insectivora (insect eaters) order is much larger, with more than 300 species. Some of its more familiar members are the shrews, moles and hedgehogs. All the species in the order—with the exception of the elephant shrew—are characterized by short legs and small eyes.

The Chiroptera (hand-wings) is an order consisting of the 900 species of bats, some of which are shown on pages 38 and 39. Bats are the only mammals that can truly fly. The other "flying" mammals such as the phalanger and flying squirrel are really gliders; bats, however, have true wings and can sustain themselves in flight; their skeletons (*page 15*), like a bird's, are extremely light, which keeps weight to a minimum. Except for the rodents, there are more species of bats than of any other order of mammals.

One of nature's oddest looking mammals

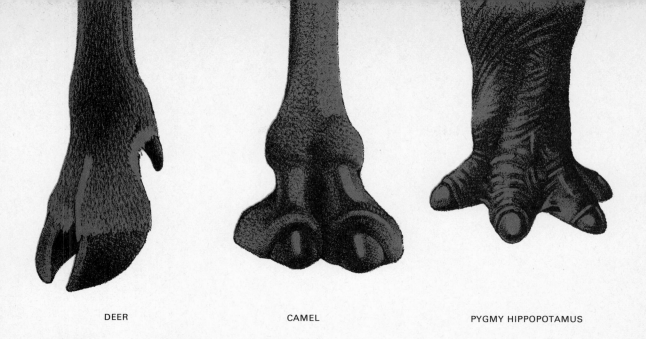

DEER   CAMEL   PYGMY HIPPOPOTAMUS

is the aardvark, found only in southern Africa. The beast, the only member of the Tubulidentata order, has big, rabbitlike ears and a long piglike snout. (The word aardvark comes from the Dutch for "earth pig.") The aardvark finds its meals in anthills and termite nests, uncovering the nests with its strong digging claws and poking its long sticky tongue in to gather up the insects.

Another curious group is the Pholidota, consisting of the seven species of pangolins. From a distance these mammals look like reptiles, for they are covered head to toe with what appear to be a reptile's scales. Close inspection reveals these "scales" to be hard, horny plates made up of hair that is closely packed and stuck together.

The name pangolin is derived from the Malay expression *pen-goling*, which means "roller." This describes the animal's habit of rolling into a tight ball when asleep or when frightened. This action protects the soft unarmored belly, leaving only the horny plates exposed, and turns the pangolin into a self-contained fortress, difficult for an enemy to penetrate.

The next order, the Edentata, includes 30 species of armadillos, sloths and anteaters. Although the scientific name for the order means toothless ones, many species do indeed have teeth. That is because scientists did not realize at first that the toothed creatures belonged to this order; by the time they knew, the order had its name. One species—the giant armadillo—possesses as many as 100 teeth. The sloths, of which there are seven species, also have teeth. In fact, only the anteaters are toothless. These mammals of Latin America have sharp digging claws for uncovering the termite mounds and anthills on which they feed.

Secrets Revealed by the Skull

The outward appearance of mammals is no guide to whether or not they are related. The two gliding mammals on this page look alike, but their skulls —particularly their teeth—reveal that they are different creatures. The phalanger has the small teeth of an insect eater; the squirrel has powerful front teeth for gnawing open nuts and seeds and broad back teeth for grinding the kernels. The mammals on the opposite page do not look alike. Yet, their similar skulls and teeth prove that all are in the order Carnivora—the meat eaters.

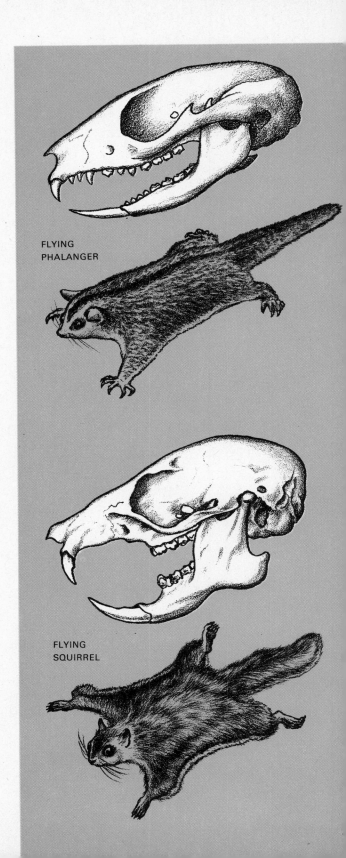

FLYING
PHALANGER

FLYING
SQUIRREL

18

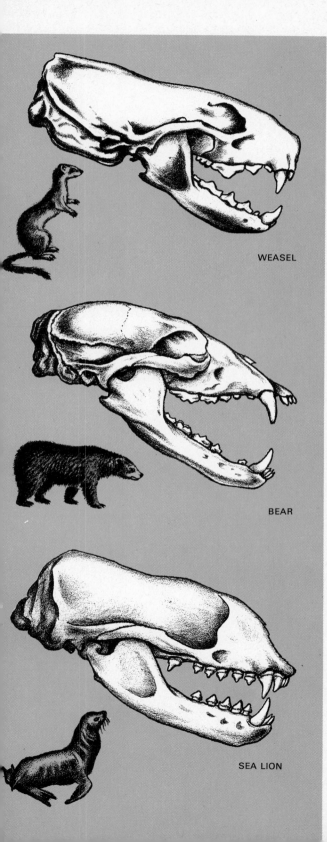

WEASEL

BEAR

SEA LION

The rodents (order Rodentia) are the most numerous of all mammalian orders, with about 1,700 species. Most rodents are small animals, some of which produce large litters with great frequency. All have sharp front teeth (*page 73*) for gnawing. The various species of rats and mice are the most familiar of all rodents, followed by the tree squirrels, of which there are about 200 species found in most parts of the globe. Closely related to squirrels, although they live on the ground rather than in trees, are the marmots, found in many parts of Europe, Asia and North America. The largest of all rodents is the capybara, a kind of outsized guinea pig from South America that sometimes grows to a length of more than three feet and can weigh 160 pounds.

The 60 species of pikas, rabbits and hares that form the order Lagomorpha (literally, "hare-shaped") closely resemble the rodents. They differ mainly in the fact that they have two sets of upper front cutting teeth instead of the single set of the rodents. Most members of this order are also characterized by their long ears and well developed hind legs, which make them highly efficient runners.

The order Carnivora, meaning meat eaters, consists of 275 species. Among them are cats, dogs, hyenas, bears, weasels, mongooses, raccoons, coatis, pandas, seals, skunks and sea lions.

The cat family includes a wide variety of highly efficient carnivores, ranging from the house cat to the lion and tiger. The teeth of cats are admirably designed for stabbing and biting the prey on which they feed. Cats hunt by careful stalking, followed by a sudden rush at their victims, a sequence familiar to anyone who has watched a pet cat stalk a sparrow.

The dogs also make up a varied group but their pattern of life differs greatly from that of cats. Dogs and their kin, such as wolves, are on the whole more sociable than cats and commonly live in packs. Several members of the dog family, such as jackals, do little hunting and feed almost entirely on dead animals.

The aquatic meat eaters, such as the seals and their close relatives, are well adapted for life in the water, for their arms and legs

Horns That Last a Lifetime

Horns are permanent growths on some mammals. On the bighorn ram they appear when the male is about eight weeks old. They grow rapidly the first year, but more slowly as the ram ages. Each year new growth appears at the base, pushing the tips out, until they twist around into a coil. It is sometimes possible to tell a ram's age from these ridges, but after a few years they may be too wrinkled to be counted.

2 YEARS   6 YEARS   12 YEARS

have been modified over the ages into flippers to help them swim.

Efficient sea beasts though they are, sea lions and seals are no match for the 80 species of whales and porpoises that make up the order Cetacea. Although often mistaken for fish because of their streamlined shape, these creatures are all warm-blooded air breathers that suckle their young. Thus they are true mammals.

The next three orders of mammals, although dissimilar in appearance, are actually fairly closely related. The five species of hyraxes (order Hyracoidea) are small, active creatures from Africa and the Middle East. The two main forms live in burrows and in trees; both look something like woodchucks. The five species of manatees and dugongs of the order Sirenia are, by contrast, large,

Antlers That Appear Each Year

Antlers, unlike horns, form and drop off every year. In the male white-tailed deer (*below*) they push out from the skull in early spring. They are not fully developed until the fall. While growing, the antlers are covered with a soft tissue called velvet. As the mating season approaches, the buck rubs off the velvet and polishes the antlers against tree trunks. In midwinter the antlers fall off, one at a time.

JUNE SEPTEMBER JANUARY

21

sluggish water-dwelling mammals that live close to shore in tropical seas. Elephants (order Proboscidea) are too well known to need an introduction; there are two species, the big-eared, sway-backed African elephant and the small-eared, humpbacked beast that lives in Asia.

Hoofed mammals are divided into two orders; those with an odd number of toes (Perissodactyla) and those having an even number (Artiodactyla). Sometimes both orders are spoken of together as ungulates, a word derived from the Latin for hoof. The odd-toed group includes horses, tapirs and rhinoceroses. The even-toed order has many more species. Many of the domestic farm mammals—cattle, sheep, pigs, goats—are in the Artiodactyla order; so are a number of wild creatures such as giraffes, okapis, antelopes, gazelles, and the many species of deer. There are only 15 species of odd-toed mammals but 170 species in the even-toed order.

Finally there is the order of primates, and among its 192 species are man and his relatives—the monkeys and apes. The word primate comes from the Latin for first, and the title reflects man's belief that any classification that includes him must be first in importance. Other members of that order, particularly the four species of great apes, exhibit a degree of reasoning power that reflects their kinship to humans. But the lemurs, also included in the order, show no great mental abilities.

These then are the orders of mammals found on earth today. They are the descendants of a much larger group, mammals that have disappeared because they were unable to meet the challenges of life on a changing planet. Some of these extinct beasts have left their mark on today's varieties. For example, the horse has certain bones that remain from the time when its ancestors had more than one toe; they do not give the beast any particular advantage, but are left over from an ancestral animal. Other extinct mammals have left no comparable identifying marks on contemporary creatures, but some have left behind their fossil remains—bones and imprints on rocks—from which zoologists have been able to piece together much of the history of mammalian evolution.

A Tiny Champion Leaper

The powerful hind legs seen in this skeleton of a jerboa show why the tiny animal is one of the greatest jumpers among mammals. Only a foot long, this rodent can vault up to 10 feet, making it an elusive target for predators. Jerboas sometimes walk on all fours; usually they leap only on their hind limbs.

2

A Long, Slow Move up Evolution's Ladder

The almost endless variety of shapes and sizes of mammals makes it difficult to remember that all mammals—elephants and mice, antelope and whales—are cousins under the skin. But to anyone who has studied their structures, it is clear that they are related, despite the fact that millions of years of evolution have shaped and molded each species into its own unique form.

What exactly is this process—evolution —and how does it work?

Although the idea of evolution was not new when Charles Darwin stated his theory in 1859, his explanation was so well thought out that it has not been successfully challenged since that time.

Darwin, after thinking over the work of earlier naturalists and his own studies, finally reached his historic conclusion in a book entitled *On the Origin of Species by Means of Natural Selection*. The theory of evolution as he stated it says, in brief, that all living things are members of a great family tree from which have sprouted hundreds of thousands of separate branches. Some branches have withered and died in the past because they did not change with altered

THE FIRST MAMMAL was probably a creature like this rat-sized *Melanodon*, which lived in North America 160 million years ago. *Melanodon* is thought to have eaten insects. One of the few early mammal fossils that have been found, this creature's remains have given clues to the origin of mammals.

25

conditions. The branches that are still alive are those that did change. The vital process through which some forms of life disappear and others survive under changing conditions was called "natural selection" by Darwin. What this means is that the challenges of life weed out the less fit and select or favor those that are better adapted.

According to the latest information, the world is about four and a half billion years old. But life in even its simplest forms may be only half that old. Scientists believe that

OPOSSUM

OXYAENA

PHENACODUS

MESONYX

TETONIUS

METACHEIROMYS

EOBASILEUS

The First Great Age of Mammals

In a painting based on fossils, early mammals wander through a North American forest some 50 million years ago. These are the ancestors of many animals common today, but most are long extinct. In the center is eohippus, an early horse the size of a small dog. Beside it grazes the giant *Uintatherium*, the forerunner of many hoofed animals. At far left, *Oxyaena*, ancestor of modern meat eaters, stalks an opossum, sole survivor into modern times.

   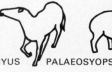

EOHIPPUS   TRITEMNODON   UINTATHERIUM   CORYPHODON   PARAMYS HYRACHYUS   PALAEOSYOPS

chemical reactions on the shores of early rivers or seas created the first tiny one-celled organisms. As generations passed, multicelled forms of life came into being, put roots down and finally turned into plants.

In a similar way, other simple organisms evolved into creatures we call animals. First came the one-celled protozoans, then very simple multicelled forms, followed by more complex animals. Then backboned creatures —such as fish, amphibians and reptiles— evolved, and finally the mammals and the birds arrived.

For the mammals, the tale begins some 180 million years ago. At that time reptiles were the dominant vertebrates. Dinosaurs, large and small, ranged over the land. Huge water-dwelling reptiles called ichthyosaurs and plesiosaurs swam in the seas. Weird leather-winged reptiles—the pterosaurs— took to the air.

Hard as it may be to believe, all mammals living today, including men, are direct descendants of reptiles. And this fact leads immediately to the question: how did reptiles evolve into mammals? What were the ani-

Oddities That Disappeared

As mammals evolved, these four strange-looking animals died out, leaving no modern offspring. *Epigaulus*, a horned rodent, lived in burrows; how it used its horns remains a puzzle. The deerlike *Syndyoceras* had two pairs of horns—one set curved in and the other out. *Alticamelus* was over 10 feet tall and browsed on trees. *Paraceratherium*, dwarfing the outline of a man, was the largest land mammal ever, measuring 25 feet long and 18 feet high.

ALTICAMELUS

SYNDYOCERAS

EPIGAULUS

PARACERATHERIUM

29

mal "bridges" between the two and what did they look like?

Because evolution is infinitely slow, there is no exact moment that can be pinpointed as the time when the first mammal was born. However, certain steps in the development of mammals can be traced. An important advance occurred in the creatures known as pelycosaurs, which lived some 280 million years ago. These beasts, which looked like lizards, had one trait that later became characteristic of mammals: instead of teeth of

 MEGATHERIUM    DIRE WOLF    BISON    SABER-TOOTHED TIGER   EQUUS

The Mammals of America in 1,000,000 B.C.

Many living North American mammals flourished as early as the great Age of Mammals, some million years ago. Seen here are various species that lived in different parts of the continent during glacial times. Many kinds, like the horse *Equus*, have much the same form today. Among those that have vanished are the towering mastodon and the equally huge woolly mammoth, the 20-foot ground sloth *Megatherium* and the giant beaver *Castoroides*.

CASTOROIDES

CAMELOPS   DOEDICURUS

MASTODON   WOOLLY MAMMOTH

MYLODON

uniform size and shape, the teeth of pelycosaurs were evolving into something like the mammalian teeth known as incisors, canines and molars.

Sometime later, a group of reptiles called therapsids evolved from the pelycosaurs. These had even more of the characteristics later found in mammals. Their skulls and teeth had a greater resemblance to those of mammals than to reptiles. Their limbs, instead of splaying out to each side of the body in a reptilian manner, were closer to the body, allowing them to move faster.

The fossil record is slightly more informative about Melanodon, a creature biologists think may have been the first true mammal (*page 24*). From the few remains that have been discovered—mainly teeth and jaws—we know that these earliest mammals were no bigger than rats. They probably lived in trees in which they did their nighttime hunting for insects. Treetop life is difficult for any animal. For one thing, the beast must have well-coordinated muscles to keep from tumbling from his perch. These distant ancestors of modern mammals started on the evolutionary road that led to the complex brains and nervous systems that characterize the higher orders of mammals today.

When these earliest mammals came into being, they were probably the underdogs in a world where reptiles reigned supreme. Then, some 60 million years ago, the pattern of life began to change. For reasons that are not fully understood almost all the great reptiles became extinct, after dominating the earth for 170 million years. The disappearance of the reptiles left a gap that mammals, with their ability to maintain an even body temperature, their advanced brains and different methods of bearing and rearing their young, were quick to fill.

The period of time during which all this took place is known as the Age of Mammals. It is an age that continues today, though

MAMMUTHUS   ELEPHAS

it might be more appropriate to label the present as the Age of Man.

Students of the earth's history divide the Age of Mammals into seven periods. The first, called the Paleocene, ended about 58 million years ago. During this period much more of the earth's surface was tropical or temperate in climate than is the case today. Plants that now grow only in the hottest tropics were found, during the Paleocene, in areas as far north as the northern United States. Even within the arctic circle a rich variety of plants grew.

Under such attractive circumstances the mammals began to spread over the face of the earth. By the dawn of the next period —the Eocene—all the main orders of mammals were flourishing, though the individual species were very different from those that exist today *(pages 26 and 27)*.

Among the mammals of the Eocene was a group known as creodonts (a very suitable

A Long Line of Elephants

Nearly 58 million years of elephant evolution march across these pages, from the pig-sized *Moeritherium* to the Asian *Elephas maximus*, one of two species still living. (The second, the African elephant, is not shown.) *Gomphotherium* had four tusks and a stumpy trunk. *Gnathobelodon* had but two tusks and a spoon-shaped lower lip. *Stegodon* was the first modern elephant. *Mammuthus*, largest of all, emerged along with today's elephants about a million years ago, but disappeared some 10,000 years ago.

name, derived from the Greek for "flesh teeth"). The creodonts, ancestors of modern meat-eating mammals, had evolved from early insect eaters; now, they were evolving in a manner that enabled them to hunt larger and more varied game.

These early flesh eaters preyed on all sorts of vegetarian mammals. Among the most spectacular of the plant eaters were those called the titanotheres, or gigantic beasts. Looking something like a rhinoceros, these monster mammals sometimes grew to be 15 feet long and eight feet high at the shoulders and had massive horns on their heads.

Also during the Eocene epoch, a familiar mammal of today first began to evolve: eohippus ("dawn horse"), a creature about the size of a fox terrier, then roamed the tropical forests. The elephants also emerged at that time, but they looked very different *(pages 32 and 33)* from today's ponderous pachyderms, for they were the size of a large pig and had not yet developed a trunk.

But of all the Eocene mammals the tree dwellers known as primates were the ones with the greatest significance for the future. Many different tree-dwelling mammals were already in existence. Small, with very well-developed brains and flexible grasping fingers, they were not yet true monkeys, but the primates of the Eocene age were slowly evolving toward the species known today.

The next epoch was the Oligocene, which began about 36 million years ago and lasted some 11 million years. During this period,

the eohippus evolved into a different and larger animal, somewhat closer to the horse we know; the elephants began to develop trunks. Similar advances were shown by many other species during the Oligocene period, and this epoch set the stage for the "golden age" of mammals—the Miocene, which began about 25 million years ago.

The Miocene was a time of tremendous change on earth. Massive movements within the earth buckled the surface of the planet and created such great mountain ranges as the Alps in Europe and the Himalayas in Asia. As the earth heaved and collapsed, new boundaries appeared between land and sea. Along with these great changes in the land came great changes in climate. The tropical zones shrank; the temperate zones became larger.

Vast herds of plant-eating mammals were grazing in the Miocene plains and forests. In addition to several kinds of horses, there were rhinos, giant pigs, the first deer with antlers, camels, llamas and ancestral giraffes. Elephants of this time had a number of sizes and shapes.

A variety of meat eaters, each adapted to hunting a different kind of victim, preyed on the grazing mammals. Early cats, dogs and bears flourished. The most spectacular of the Miocene carnivores was the "saber-toothed tiger" *(page 30)*. This cat had a pair of enormously long upper teeth, probably used to slash through the thick hide of the mastodon, a kind of elephant. Late in the

Patient Helper of Man

A common land mammal, the donkey has been a servant to man for over 5,000 years. This creature lived originally in Africa, and as the land grew drier, it moved into Palestine, Syria and Asia. It was first tamed in the Nile Valley and is now found on all continents except Antarctica.

Aquatic Mammals

Some mammals, like the manatee
(*near right*) and the walrus (*far right*),
long ago returned to a life in water.
There the walrus's four limbs evolved
into flippers. The manatee's hind limbs
were replaced by a flattened tail;
the front limbs became flippers. Two
other mammals, the whales and
porpoises, have adapted so well to
the water that they look like fish.

Miocene epoch, mammals began to decline, and a number of species became extinct. This decline continues even today. The only groups to escape this decline were the primates, rodents and bats, which still continue their successful evolutionary course.

Apes were already swinging through the Asian and European forests some 20 million years ago. The ancestors of various species of monkeys flourished during the same time. In East Africa an interesting great ape, *Proconsul*, thrived. This creature may have been very close to the early forms of the chimpanzee; in fact it may have been part of the line through which man himself evolved.

In spite of the decline of mammalian life after the Miocene, the next two epochs, the Pliocene and the Pleistocene, continued to be characterized by an enormous variety of mammals. In the early Pliocene, giraffes were numerous and included short-necked forms as well as the long-necked species of today. A strange, deerlike beast, *Synthetoceras* had a huge Y-forked horn behind its nostrils as well as conventional horns sprouting from its forehead. South America was inhabited by several giant creatures whose living cousins today are of small or moderate size. A huge ground sloth, for instance, was as big as an elephant, and enormous creatures looking like armadillos roamed the land.

The Pleistocene, the epoch before the present one, was a particularly harsh time. Four times in the last million years great sheets of ice, glaciers, have advanced from the polar regions to cover much of the earth, driving practically all life before them and then slowly receding. The last withdrawal of the glaciers occurred only 10,000 years ago and continues today.

Some of the mammals of the glacial ages (*pages 30 and 31*) made very effective adaptations to these harsh conditions. Thus, cousins of several creatures that now are quite hairless were characterized in the early Pleistocene by thick, warm coats of hair. The so-called "woolly mammoth" is a famous ex-

ample of an ice-age mammal that made this particular adaptation to the cold. A woolly rhinoceros, living in the same regions as the mammoth, was also protected by a furry coat; today's rhinos are almost hairless. Although hair is not normally preserved in fossil form, we know of its existence in these mammals because the remains of their bodies have been dug up—shaggy coats and all —from the permanently frozen arctic soil.

Many other species of mammals, however, were killed off in the great ice ages, either by the cold, or—in more temperate areas— by the crowding and competition of other species or by the most skillful hunter of all

—man. But even without the danger from man. But even without the danger from man, many of the species that once roamed the earth would have perished. The amazing thing is that, in the face of repeated cycles of glacial advance and freezing cold, so many species managed to survive. The reason they did can be found by studying the process of natural selection.

When an animal's surroundings change, the creature must move to a new area similar to the old or adapt. Eohippus, the little dawn horse, had teeth adapted only for chewing fairly soft food, a fact that suggests it lived on the tender shoots of the forest rather than the tough grasses of the plains. Two factors forced eohippus from the forests to the plains: the ice ages reduced the size of heavily wooded areas and increased

Bats: A Large and Unique Order

The 12 kinds of South American bats shown above
are a small sampling of the 900 or so species found
around the world, making them the second largest
mammalian order after rodents. While flying squirrels
and some other mammals can glide from a high perch,
only bats are capable of true flapping-wing flight.
Their wings, made of thin membranes of skin stretched
between their elongated fingers and their bodies,
enable them to maneuver with birdlike grace.

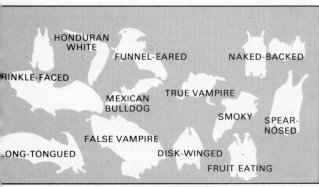

HONDURAN
WHITE

FUNNEL-EARED   NAKED-BACKED

RINKLE-FACED

MEXICAN   TRUE VAMPIRE
BULLDOG

SMOKY   SPEAR-
NOSED

FALSE VAMPIRE

ONG-TONGUED   DISK-WINGED

FRUIT-EATING

the competition for plant food in those forests that remained, and new breeds of meat-eating predators with appetites for horseflesh now hunted in the woods.

When eohippus moved onto the plains, larger and faster individuals had a better chance for survival, for they could see over the tall grasses to spot predators and could run quickly enough to escape. The smaller, slower horses were eventually destroyed by their enemies, while the larger horses thrived, reproduced and multiplied. These successful horses passed on the tendency toward large size and high speed to their descendants; the former tendency to smallness and slowness disappeared. Another change arising out of altered habits was the modification in the horse's teeth, which were now adapted to chewing coarse plains grasses.

Elephant evolution (*pages 32 and 33*) differed in detail, though the principle of natural selection remained the same. The early, small swamp-dwelling elephants disappeared when faced with a changing climate, but those that had developed new characteristics suitable to life in drier conditions survived.

In these new circumstances, increased size became an advantage, for it helped in resisting attack by predators in open country. For defense the elephant also relied on its tusks and an exceptionally thick skin. A short neck made it easier to support the heavy weight of its tusks. But hampered by the short neck and fenced off by long tusks, the elephant could not reach the ground to graze. The answer to this problem is seen in the development of a long upper lip and nose, or trunk, which could both reach the ground and extend upward beyond the tusks.

Many mammals, however, were much less successful at adapting than horses and elephants. In fact, the species living today are only a small percentage of all the species that have ever lived. Extinction rather than survival is likely to be the fate of most species. This is not surprising considering the many natural and, lately, man-made impediments each species must overcome. Whether or not today's species continue to live depends entirely upon their ability to adapt to the demands of the new challenges that most certainly will arise.

A Living Relic of the Past

The white rhinoceros, resembling an extinct giant of the past, may itself be headed for extinction. However, unlike its ancestors, which were overcome by predators or changing climates, this once plentiful mammal has been cut down by man. Surviving specimens are protected in game preserves and zoos.

3

A Variety of Methods for Getting About

The speed, agility and physical power with which an animal moves as it seeks out food or escapes from enemies plays a large role in determining its chances for survival. We are all familiar with such phrases as "the thundering herd of buffalo," "the stalking cat," "the bounding gazelle" and "the lumbering elephant," which describe the movements of these mammals—movements that give each an advantage over less favored creatures in the battle for life. In fact, an important reason why mammals are one of the earth's dominant groups is that they are more mobile than any other group of ground-dwelling creatures. There are even mammals that have invaded the air and sea to compete successfully with the birds and fishes.

The great majority of mammals are classified as "tetrapods," which means four-footed. Mammals are the descendants of finned fishes that, countless millions of years ago, came up on shore to seek out a new life as land dwellers. Helping these fish to adapt to life in their new surroundings was the fact that they could, with difficulty, use four of their fins for movement on land. Eventually these fins evolved into legs with feet

RED KANGAROOS, a mother and her baby (called a joey), lounge idly, supported by their tails and hind legs. Kangaroos use their tails as a prop when walking or standing. But when hurrying, they make leaps of up to 25 feet, their heads stretched well forward—and their tails stretched out behind for balance.

—characteristics common to all their descendants, the amphibians, reptiles, birds and mammals.

Mammals as different in size and shape as the mouse and the hippopotamus, the chamois and the giraffe, the buffalo and the squirrel all share the ability to run or walk on four legs. But there are exceptions. The kangaroos (*pages 42, 44 and 45*) and the little rodents called jerboas occasionally walk on all fours, but generally they leap with their powerful hind limbs; their long tails help them to maintain balance. In contrast, several species of monkeys and apes move about mainly by swinging with their front limbs. These forelimbs—or arms—are much better adapted to swinging through the treetops than to walking on the ground. As another example, there is man, whose dominance over other animal life is based—at least in some measure—on his manner of locomotion. By walking on his hind limbs he leaves his forelimbs free for toolmaking and other uses.

By and large, however, mammals are designed to walk or run on all four feet. The horse provides a good example of how a typical tetrapod moves. To begin a walk, the horse may step off by raising his right forefoot. This is followed by the left hind foot, then the left forefoot and finally the right hind foot. The cycle is then immediately repeated, and the horse moves forward at a leisurely rate, always resting on three of its four feet.

The walk, however, is too slow to meet many of the challenges of daily life; walking would be of no use to a horse trying to escape from a lion, for example. A little faster than a walk is the trot. Though the feet move in the same sequence of steps as in a walk, in each cycle there is a brief instant when the animal is supported by only two of its four limbs. Therefore, while the trot is speedier than the walk, it is less steady.

When horses, cats, dogs and many other

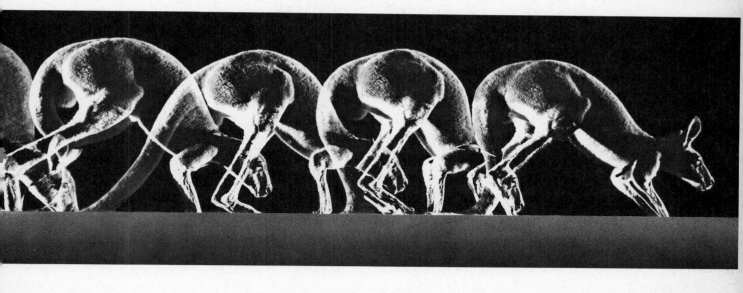

A Kangaroo in Low and High Gear

Multiple-exposure photographs reveal how the kangaroo walks *(above)* and hops *(below)*. The walk starts *(exposure at left, above)* with the animal's weight on the hind legs. Then the kangaroo balances on its tail and front legs. It swings its hind legs and body forward, almost like a man on crutches, and then repeats the cycle. Hopping *(below)*, the kangaroo springs forward on its hind legs, keeping its forefeet off the ground. These pictures catch the animal swinging its legs ahead while its body is in mid-air, a motion creating spurts of speed of up to 30 miles per hour.

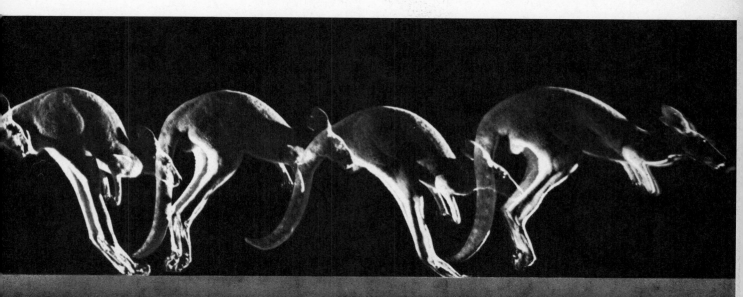

Cumbersome, but Fast

Rumbling across an African plain, a black rhinoceros moves his bulky body with surprising speed and agility. Weighing as much as 4,000 pounds, this animal can speed along at 30 miles per hour for short stretches and can change direction quickly enough to discourage many of its attackers.

mammals trot, they usually raise the two legs that are diagonally opposite—the left front and the right hind together and the right front and the left hind together. But certain other mammals follow a different sequence. The camel and elephant lift the legs on the same side at the same time. This produces a gait called the pace, which gives these animals a peculiar rolling motion. People who ride an elephant or camel for the first time often become slightly ill, for the motion produces something akin to seasickness.

Running as fast as it can, a tetrapod mammal is said to be galloping. In the gallop three of the feet—and often all four—are off the ground at certain points in the cycle. This type of movement by a horse is illustrated on pages 48 and 49; the gait is also used by such different species as hares and weasels. When it gallops, a horse lifts its limbs in a different order from that used for walking; the sequence is right front, left front, right hind, left hind. At times, because of the rapidity with which the feet are

raised, the horse flies through the air with no support whatsoever. And the distance covered in each sequence of steps is great. The imprints of the same hoof may be as much as 25 feet apart—four times the length of the animal's body.

During a gallop the horse's backbone remains comparatively rigid; the muscles of the legs provide almost all the power for forward motion. The cheetah, a big member of the cat family, adds to the power of its gallop in a special way. Fastest of all mammals, the cheetah is able to bend its spine as if it were a spring. The power released as the spine straightens out gives the animal added forward movement through the legs (*above and opposite*). With this advantage the cheetah can whiz along for short periods at more than 70 miles per hour.

Even more remarkable than the cheetah's top speed is its ability to accelerate, or speed up. From a standing start it can reach 45 miles per hour in two seconds, a performance that might make the fastest sports car look as though it was standing still. A num-

ber of other mammals travel at high speeds: the African wildebeest, the springbok and Thomson's and Grant's gazelles can rocket along at 50 miles per hour, and even the seemingly ponderous Cape buffalo is able to charge at 35 miles per hour.

Speed is largely dependent on leg and foot structure. The feet of slow mammals, such as bears and primates, are large, weight-bearing surfaces. When such animals walk, the entire foot is in contact with the ground during part of the time, and they are known as "plantigrade," a word made up from the Latin for "sole of the foot" and "to walk."

Faster mammals, such as the dog and cat, are known as "digitigrade"; they stand and walk on their toes, or digits, with the heel permanently raised off the ground.

The fastest group as a whole is the category that includes the horses, antelopes and gazelles, called the "unguligrade." This means that they move along on the very tips of their toenails, which are the growths called hoofs.

While it may seem that the fastest mammals are better equipped to deal with life, this is not always the case. It all depends on where and how the animal lives. Thus the slender limbs of the horse, combined with the large muscles of its chest and hips, make the animal a speedster on flat, dry surfaces, where it can easily outdistance the slow-footed bear. But on an icy road the horse may slip and slide as it strives to maintain its balance. On the same frozen surface, a bear's broad-soled feet give it a firm grasp. The bear is therefore much less likely to lose its balance and come tumbling down in a heap. Instead it plods along at a steady though not very rapid pace, or, in the words of the old saying, it "makes haste slowly."

The mountain sheep and mountain goats that scramble up nearly sheer cliffs on all-but-invisible ledges have feet especially well adapted for their life in rugged terrain. Their hoofs have sharp edges and the undersides curve in. The sharp edges give them a "toe-hold" on rocky slopes, while the slightly

Speeding with a Springy Spine

Despite its smaller size and shorter legs, a cheetah can sprint faster than a horse because it possesses a highly flexible backbone. The drawings above show how the cheetah can bend its backbone like a spring, allowing it to bring its hind legs well forward and giving it a long stride. When the spine is straightened, its action adds to the push of the powerful hind legs. Cheetahs do not have much endurance and, over a long course, will be outrun by the level-running horse.

49

cupped hoofs grip the ground. In the Arctic, mammals as different as the polar bear, the Canada lynx and the well-named snowshoe hare have big, broad, flat feet that keep them from sinking into the snow; furry soles keep them from slipping.

Although man is unique among mammals in developing and perfecting the two-legged stance, there are several other mammals that have tended in this direction. Kangaroos, for example, exhibit one of the most specialized gaits in the animal kingdom (*pages 44 and 45*). When walking, the kangaroo uses not four supporters but five, for the thick muscular tail acts as a fifth limb. Starting with all four feet and its tail on the ground, the kangaroo lifts up its two hind limbs, leaving its weight on its short front legs and the tail. The hind legs swing forward to a new resting place to be followed by the forelimbs.

As the kangaroo starts going faster than a walk, a different movement takes over—the familiar leaping gait for which they are famous. Now, only the hind limbs come in contact with the ground. The body leans well forward and is balanced by the tail, which stretches out behind. The long, powerful hind legs push the animal forward at speeds up to 30 miles per hour. On occasion, kangaroos have been seen to jump, in a single leap, 40 feet forward and as high as eight feet in the air.

The Old World jerboas as well as the New World kangaroo rats and jumping mice leap very much like miniature kangaroos. Their hind limbs are even longer in proportion to their forelimbs than are those of kangaroos, and their tails are likewise used for balance.

A few mammals, such as moles and pocket gophers, spend practically their entire lives underground. Both have short, power-

ful forelimbs equipped with strong claws for digging, and the entire forelimbs of moles are broadened and flattened into highly efficient shovels.

A much larger number of mammals have, in whole or in part, given up life on the ground for a new kind of existence in the leafy world of the treetops. In these new surroundings of swaying branches the tail becomes an important organ. Generally it is used for balance. But for some monkeys it is like a fifth grasping "hand." The long-tailed pangolin of Africa, certain monkeys and the opossums all use their tails as supporting "hands." There are some monkeys, such as the spider monkey, the woolly monkey and the howler, that can easily support the entire weight of their bodies with their tails.

Another change in tree-dwelling mammals is in the structure of their limbs. Among tree-dwelling primates there is a tendency for the

Follow the Leader, Monkey Style

Howler monkeys of the tropical American rain forests move along a branch on all fours in search of food. They use their flexible tails as a fifth limb, grasping one branch as they swing to the next. On the march, they often take the same route and follow the same order, a large adult male leading the way and another guarding the rear. Here a youngster has bounded ahead, but it will soon drop back behind the leader.

51

A School of Playful Swimmers

Dolphins, churning the waters in the Gulf of California, are a highly specialized type of swimming mammal. Many land mammals can swim if they have to, and others, such as beavers, have webbed feet that help in swimming. Dolphins, however, are built only for life at sea and can not move on land.

hind limbs to become heavier and stronger than the forelimbs. This is because the hind limbs are needed to support the body weight, while the forelimbs, like arms, reach about in search of new places to hold on to.

Many tree-dwelling mammals also have an opposable thumb, like that possessed by human beings. The opposable thumb is valuable because it can close against the other fingers to form a kind of tongs for picking things up. In man the opposable thumb is more flexible—and therefore better adapted to grasping small objects—than in any other mammal.

Though several groups of mammals can throw themselves into the air and then glide downward for relatively short distances, the only mammals that can truly fly are the bats. Though the wing structures of bats and birds differ, the movement of their wings is similar. Both creatures move their wings downward and forward in one motion and then backward and upward in another. Bats, like birds, can glide for a short while on motionless wings, though they lack the birds' ability to soar on currents of air.

Bats, which have poor eyesight, fly mostly at night and avoid crashing into obstacles by making noises that create echoes. These echoes bounce back to the bat and act as a kind of sonar device. Ships use echoing sound waves produced by sonar apparatus to detect underwater objects. Similarly, a flying bat gives out a constant series of sounds. These bounce off nearby objects and warn the bat of things in its way. How the bat distinguishes between various kinds of echoes —for instance, between an outcropping of rock to be avoided and an insect to be caught —is not yet known.

The swimming mammals have made an adaptation that is just as extreme as that made by the bats. While all land vertebrates developed from water-dwelling ancestors, certain mammals returned to the water between 50 and 60 million years ago. They can be divided into three groups.

First there are the mammals that only occasionally take to the water. Hares, hedgehogs, dogs, mice, moles, weasels and even cats are excellent swimmers. But these are not really water mammals, and their ability to swim is based on the use of organs designed for life on the land. The hamster, for example, increases its buoyancy by filling its cheek pouches with air.

In the second group are the mammals with structures primarily adapted for water use. The webbed feet of the otter and the platypus work well on land but are especially adapted for swimming. The beaver uses its flat, blade-shaped tail as a rudder in the water; on land the tail serves as a brace when the beaver sits up to gnaw on a tree.

The third group, true water mammals, are those that have become most highly specialized for aquatic life. These include the sea cows, the whales, the porpoises and the seals and their relatives. Although their ancestors were four-footed land animals, water mammals have become so at home in the water that many of them have lost the ability to move about on land.

In the course of the evolution of these water mammals, various species developed different uses for their limbs. Walruses and seals may use all four webbed feet to propel themselves through the water, although the seals often swim on their backs and paddle with their hind limbs alone. Elephant seals also swim with their hind limbs, but sea lions depend mainly on their forelimbs for propulsion and use their rear limbs for steering.

The sea cows are so thoroughly adapted for a water existence that they have lost their hind limbs entirely. Seen at a distance, sea cows look somewhat like the mermaids described in legend; through the centuries, imaginative sailors who have caught sight of sea cows have brought back tales of having sighted mermaids. However, if any of these voyagers had seen a sea cow close up, he could never have confused its wrinkled, hairy face with that of a beautiful girl.

Whales and dolphins are the most specialized of all water mammals. In fact, they have developed so many fishlike structures —such as fins and torpedo-shaped bodies— that they are sometimes mistaken for fish. As with sea cows, the hind limbs have been lost, though many species do retain small bony remnants of these limbs buried deep in their flesh. These bones seem to serve no useful function, and it is likely that eventually they will disappear altogether. The forelimbs of whales turned into fins, which are used mainly for steering; whales propel themselves through the water with powerful up-and-down strokes of their tails.

These are only a few examples of how the limbs of mammals and the manner in which they use them are connected with their ways of life. Every animal that has pursued a successful evolutionary course has done so because it has been able to adapt to the challenges posed by the changing surroundings in which it lives. It is not by accident that a whale has fins while a monkey has fingers and a horse has hooves. These organs all give their owners a better chance of success in the continuing contest that allows only the "survival of the fittest."

Fluttering, Flapping Fliers

Bats, like these streaming out of a Texas cave, are the only true flying mammals. Other so-called fliers, such as the flying squirrel, can only glide on broad flaps of skin stretched between front and back limbs. Compared to birds, most bats have an uneven flying motion, but can still stay aloft for hours.

4

The Wanderers and the Stay-at-Homes

MIGRATING CARIBOU cross a Canadian tundra on the way to a grazing area. Many animals have favorite locales where they spend certain seasons, traveling to and from the same areas each year.

Some species of mammals, including some humans, are stay-at-homes. They find life in their immediate neighborhoods so easy to sustain that they seldom roam more than a few hundred yards away from their burrows, caves or treetops. Other species—again like some humans—are affected by a seasonal wanderlust. These migratory mammals travel hundreds or even thousands of miles every year. Practical considerations—the need to seek out new food supplies or to flee from winter's cold or, in certain cases, to escape from overpopulation—cause them to travel. No mammal, except man, wanders merely to fulfill a sense of adventure.

Mammalian wanderings fall into two basic categories. First, there is the migration of those mammals whose journeys are dictated by the seasons. Like some birds they travel from summer to winter feeding grounds, returning to the same areas year after year.

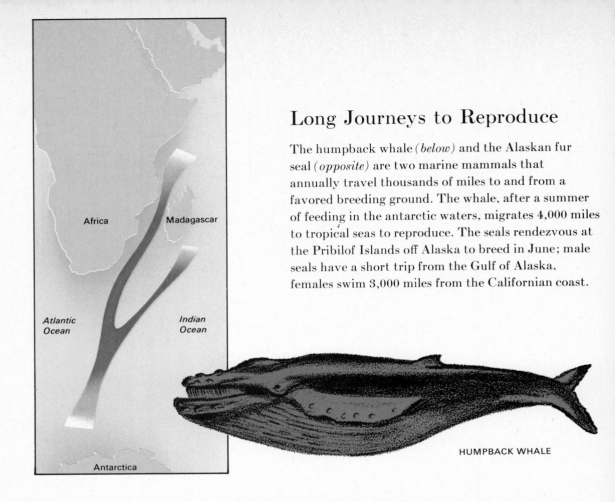

Long Journeys to Reproduce

The humpback whale (*below*) and the Alaskan fur seal (*opposite*) are two marine mammals that annually travel thousands of miles to and from a favored breeding ground. The whale, after a summer of feeding in the antarctic waters, migrates 4,000 miles to tropical seas to reproduce. The seals rendezvous at the Pribilof Islands off Alaska to breed in June; male seals have a short trip from the Gulf of Alaska, females swim 3,000 miles from the Californian coast.

HUMPBACK WHALE

Second, there are the year-round wanderings of mammals like the mountain lion of the Americas that ranges 30 to 50 miles in search of prey.

Examples of true migrations can be found among many species of mammals. Among the land dwellers, however, it is the large, hoofed species that are the most notably migratory. For example, the caribou of North America (*pages 56, 57, 66 and 67*) wander over a vast area. Their seasonal migrations may carry them as much as 400 or 500 miles from their starting points. Naturalists have long studied caribou migrations. They have found that toward the end of July, when the first chill hints of winter sweep over the

North American tundra beyond the timber line, herds of caribou begin their trek to the south. They follow the same annual routes to the sheltered evergreen forests south of the timber line. It is during this migration that breeding takes place.

The following spring the pregnant female caribou leave the males behind and move north to the summer feeding grounds on the tundra. There the females, called cows, and their young calves (some of which are born during the migration, others on the tundra) await the males, who leave the forests somewhat later. By early May the males, called bulls, appear at the feeding grounds. The reassembled herd now wanders over the tun-

ALASKAN FUR SEAL

dra, grazing until it is time to go south again.

Nothing short of disaster—the wiping out of an entire herd—can stop the caribou from making their twice-yearly migrations. They press on despite all obstacles, defying even the swollen streams, though hundreds may drown during a single crossing.

Migrating across land is a difficult and dangerous task. Flooding rivers and mountain ranges are only two of the barriers the mammal must face. However, since the sea and the air offer fewer barriers than the land, it is understandable that migration is common among many bats and sea mammals. The great blue whale, the largest animal of all time, is one sea creature that makes long

journeys. One blue whale covered a distance of 300 miles in 32 days, while another voyaged some 500 miles in 88 days.

Information about whale migration is obtained by marking individual whales. Since a whale will not stay still while a naturalist pins a marker to its hide, experts fire metal labels from guns. These tags imbed themselves in the thick blubber underneath the whale's skin. When a tagged whale is finally caught, the label is removed and sent to a central record-keeping authority. This is the way that naturalists keep track of the migrations of the enormous beasts. Journeys of more than 1,000 miles have occasionally been recorded for blue whales, although such long-distance trips seem to be unusual.

The gray whales cover even greater distances than blue whales. Their marathon journeys often take them more than 2,000 miles from their starting points. This species bears its young during the winter while inhabiting the sheltered lagoons on the coast of Lower California. With the approach of warm weather the whales begin their swim to the north. By the time summer arrives they are patrolling the North Pacific and Arctic Oceans to feed on abundant supplies of plankton, tiny aquatic organisms.

Perhaps the champion long-distance mi-

grants among whales are the humpbacks (*page 58*) of the Southern Hemisphere. During the winter these mammals breed in the tropical seas along the coasts of South America, Africa, New Zealand and Australia. But when summer arrives, they move south to the shores of the antarctic. These seasonal

Moving Day on the Prairie

Bison thunder across a Montana meadow, recalling the migrations of the past. Moving with the seasons, enormous herds grazed on the Great Plains until they were almost wiped out by 19th Century hunters.

Flourishing with Man's Help

For armadillos (*right*) and coyotes (*opposite*), the expansion of civilization in North America has brought about an increase of their ranges. For most mammals the contrary has been true. As their natural enemies were killed off by man, armadillos wandered north from Mexico to east of the Mississippi. Coyotes, despite persistent hunting by man, fed on the ever increasing herds of domestic livestock and spread across much of the continent.

ARMADILLO RANGES

migrations, made twice each year, often cover distances of up to 4,000 miles.

The fin whale is also a great traveler between antarctic and tropical waters. One individual of the species was found nearly 2,000 miles from the place where it was originally tagged.

The migrations of bats, though not nearly so long as those undertaken by many marine mammals, often carry them hundreds of miles away from their starting points. The tiny European pipistrelle bat, for example, regularly travels from southeastern Europe to the central provinces of Russia, and back again—600 to 800 miles each way. The Mexican freetail bat travels even farther; its summer home in the Tucson, Arizona, region is more than 800 miles from its winter quarters near Jalisco, Mexico.

Naturalists who study bat migrations band the forelimbs of these mammals with metal rings in the hope that someday the bat will be recaptured at its destination and the number on the band will be recorded. More often than not the hope is a futile one, for only about three bands in 100 are ever recovered. But even these few are enough to show that bats follow a constant migratory pattern.

How do mammals decide when to migrate from summer to winter feeding grounds? Do

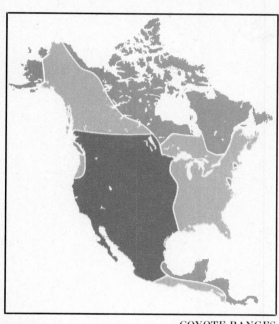

COYOTE RANGES

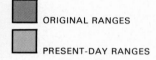

ORIGINAL RANGES

PRESENT-DAY RANGES

they think that because the weather is turning cold or hot the time has come to seek a more comfortable climate? The answer is most certainly "no." The urge to migrate, like so many other aspects of animal behavior, is based upon body chemistry. Certain physical changes, such as extra activity of various glands, tell an animal when the time has come. No act of will or thought is necessary. It would be a physical impossibility for a migratory mammal to ignore these chemical signals.

If migratory mammals are forced by their internal chemistry to migrate, how then do they find their way to the same destination year after year? They have no maps to guide

them and no compass to keep their course. Yet, most mammals, even those that do not migrate, seem to have a homing instinct. A tiny deer mouse, for example, normally wanders no more than 100 yards from its nest. Yet, when scientists moved these little creatures two miles from home, the mice sometimes were able to find their way back again. The homing of bats is even more remarkable. Some were taken 28 miles from their nesting sites and found their way back within a day. Others were captured and then set free 165 miles from home. Amazing as it may seem, some of the bats managed to find their way back, though it took them several days.

Nobody really knows how mammals manage such feats. Certainly luck must play some part. It also seems probable that a lost mammal will wander about until a familiar landmark is sighted. But these explanations cannot account for all instances of successful homing, particularly those involving the mass seasonal travels of many mammals.

Experiments with birds may throw some light on the matter. It now seems likely that migratory birds rely to some extent on the stars as navigation aids, just as sailors do. If this is true for birds, it may be true for mammals as well, particularly bats. Yet even if this is so, a mystery still remains. For while it is reasonable to suppose that migratory mammals are born with an instinct for finding their way, how this instinct operates is still an unsolved puzzle.

Migration is only one type of mammalian travel; another is emigration. Unlike the migrating mammal, the emigrating one does not return to its original home. One of the primary causes of emigration seems to be overpopulation. When there are too many animals in an area, the result is insufficient food and not enough homesites. At a certain point, the competition becomes too great and migration begins. Thus, ever since colonial times, mass emigrations of gray squirrels have been noted frequently in North America. Moving in vast numbers and devouring the wheat and corn crops in their paths, these squirrels leave behind them barren fields and angry farmers. One of the greatest of these treks occurred in Wisconsin in 1842 and lasted four weeks. Basing his

A Mass Drive to Tragedy

Plunging into water, a band of lemmings heads for probable death by drowning. They are not committing mass suicide. Instead, these rodents, pressed by population explosions, are in search of new food supplies. Rather than change course, lemmings try— and often fail—to swim across water barriers.

figures on the number of squirrels that passed a given point every hour, one eyewitness estimated that the number of squirrels involved was in the hundreds of millions.

The pressures of population and food shortage that lead to mass emigration can sometimes be helpful to a species, for it opens up new territories for colonization. Armadillos and coyotes (*pages 62 and 63*), for example, are now much more widely spread around North America than they once were. Mammals as different as the mouse and man have been successful in adjusting their lives to difficult climates and terrains. Sometimes, however, enforced emigrations have disastrous consequences for vast numbers. An example that has always

captured the imagination of scientists is the emigrations of the Norwegian lemmings.

These small rodents inhabit high plateaus and mountain slopes. For years at a time their numbers may be quite small. Then, probably because of a sudden increase in the food supply, a great population increase occurs. With plenty of food available, the lemmings reproduce at a fantastic rate. If these favorable conditions continue over several years, the population explosion begins to outstrip the food resources. When this happens, a mass emigration of the surplus population begins.

At first the lemmings travel as individuals, but natural barriers, such as rivers, create bottlenecks, and the creatures pile up on the banks, frantically seeking a safe cross-

ing (*page 64*). Eventually a mass movement into the water begins, and many thousands are drowned, but millions survive to continue the trek. Finally the survivors reach the sea. This body of water is too vast to be crossed, and the lemmings once more hesitate on the banks. But the pressure of new arrivals is so great that the ones on shore are swept forward into the sea.

Passengers on a vessel steaming in Norwegian waters once passed through a mass of swimming lemmings. Together, these millions of doomed animals formed a moving mass at least two miles wide. Moreover, this group formed only a single branch of a far greater horde whose size was impossible to estimate. Except for a few individuals lucky enough to land on an offshore island, the entire swarm was doomed. So it is with all such lemming emigrations. Yet there is a good side to these suicidal treks. Destruction of millions of these creatures re-establishes the balance between population and food supply to insure the survival of the species.

Wild Nomads of the North

A herd of about 5,000 caribou flows over the treeless Canadian tundra. After a winter south of the tree line, they hurry 400 to 500 miles northward with the coming of spring. Their calves are born in the north and make the trek south with their parents to seek the protection of the evergreen forest as fall approaches.

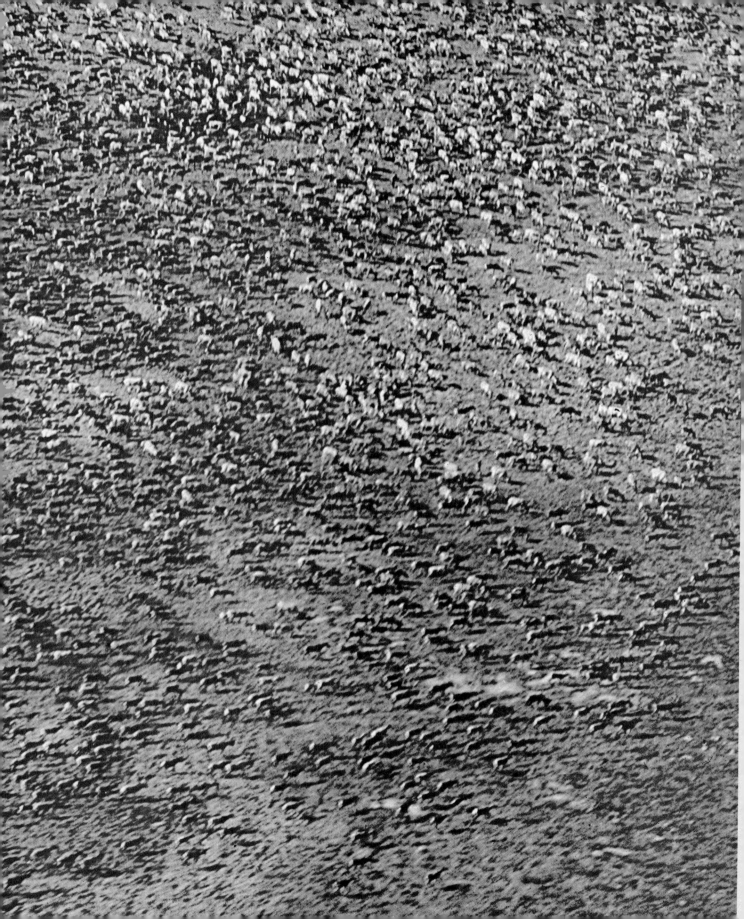

5
The Pressing Need to Find a Meal

All kinds of life need food. Without it animals and plants would quickly perish. Among the lowest animals, eating is relatively simple. An amoeba, which has only one cell, absorbs food through its membrane "skin." For higher animals such as the mammals, the process is much more complicated. The animal must first find a supply of suitable food. A lion would starve to death if the only food it could find was grass, but a horse would thrive on exactly the same food supply.

Having found something it can eat, the animal has to get the food into its mouth. Although this may sound simple, it is often very difficult. A giraffe (*page 80*), for example, can survive only in places where tender leaves and shoots of trees and shrubs grow quite high, so that they are close to the giraffe's mouth; if the giraffe always had to bend down to reach ground-level vegetation, it would be so open to attack by its enemies that it might soon perish. On the other hand, a short-necked grass eater, such as the giant sable antelope (*page 76*), would not be able to reach the tall trees on which a giraffe feeds.

Teeth to Fit the Food

Drawings of the jaws of three mammals reveal teeth shaped to match their diets. The meat-eating wolf has powerful canines for stabbing its food, and premolars and molars to shred it. The deer, a plant eater, has incisors and canines in the lower jaw and a horny pad on the upper jaw, used for cropping. The porcupine, a rodent, has enlarged incisors for gnawing, but no canines at all.

◼ INCISORS

◼ CANINES

◼ PREMOLARS AND MOLARS

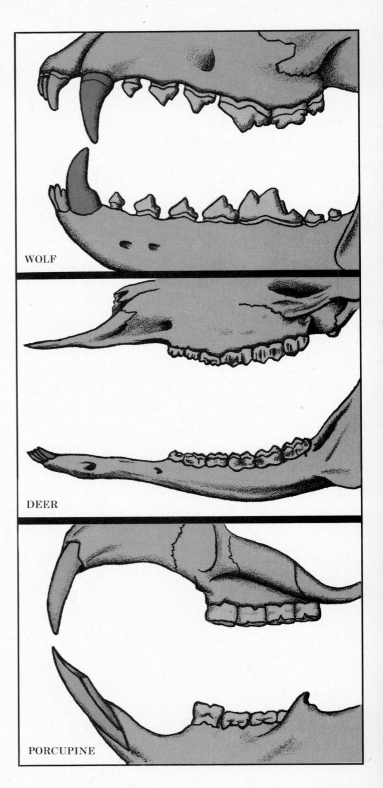

WOLF

DEER

PORCUPINE

For the meat-eating mammals, carnivores, the problems of actually securing food are doubly difficult. Except for those meat eaters, called scavengers, that prey on dead animals, carnivores must catch as well as find their prey. Some carnivorous mammals run down their prey by superior speed. Others hide in ambush or employ some other hunting tactic.

Even when food has been seized it must still be turned into useful nourishment. The animal's mouth must have suitable machinery for breaking the food into pieces small enough to swallow. In most mammals, teeth do this job very effectively. These vary in size and shape from one species to another (*opposite*).

Mammals generally have four different kinds of teeth, called incisors, canines, premolars and molars. The incisors, at the front of the jaws are normally designed for nipping, cutting and gnawing; the canines, which lie just behind the incisors, are used for seizing, stabbing and tearing; the premolars and molars at the back of the jaw are for grinding and chewing. Not all mammals have all four kinds, however, and the size, variety, number and placement of the teeth depend on a species' way of life. Every species has teeth that are especially adapted to its diet or to its needs for defense against attack by enemies.

In some mammals these adaptations have gone so far that some of the teeth no longer help the creatures to eat. The tusks of an elephant (*page 81*), for example, were originally incisor teeth, but today they have nothing to do with chewing. Instead their primary use is for attack, defense and for breaking branches from trees. Sometimes, however, the tusks do have a minor role in gathering food; elephants use them to root in the ground and uncover edible morsels buried there.

There are other specialized mouth parts that give their owners an advantage in gathering food. The long, flexible tongue of the giraffe, for example, is used to encircle and break off leaves and shoots of trees; the extremely rough tongue of the cat helps it to scrape flesh from bones; and the pointed tongue of the honey possum (*page 82*) lets it reach inside flowers to gather nectar.

When a mammal swallows food, usually after chewing it into smaller, more manageable chunks, the morsels pass through a number of internal organs. The chewed food travels from the stomach into the large and small intestines; there, chemicals and bacteria break down the food into fuel that is used to provide energy for heat and motion. Only when the necessary nourishment has been extracted from the food is it passed out of the body in the form of manure that may fertilize the soil and eventually help produce more food.

Although all mammals turn food into fuel through a similar digestive process, there are enormous differences in the diets of different species. Some mammals have danger-

EAST AFRICAN MOLE RAT   NAKED MOLE RAT

ously specialized diets. For instance, the koala of Australia, an appealing little fellow that looks like a Teddy bear, would disappear forever if a certain species of eucalyptus tree on which it feeds should die off. Similarly, the red tree mouse of the Northwestern United States eats only the needles and young shoots of the Douglas fir tree. Some bats—and some monkeys—will die of starvation rather than eat anything but certain fruits. The mustached white-nosed monkey, for example, is found only in west Central Africa, where a special kind of palm tree grows; the monkey feeds mostly on its fruit. The disadvantages of so limited a diet are obvious; if one of these species is unable to adopt new feeding habits it may face extinction when conditions change.

In general, however, most mammals can, within limits, shift from one food to another. Hunger is a great spur to trying new food. A mammal that normally would refuse a certain kind of food may accept it rather than starve. Many mammalian diets also vary considerably with the season of the year, with the animal's age and with the state of its health.

By far the greatest number of mammals are herbivores, that is, they have a vegetarian diet. Grasses, shoots and leaves are the basic foods of many vegetarian mammals, but these do not complete the list. Among other plant foods enjoyed by mammals are nectar, fruits, bark, fungi and nuts. Certain tropical bats live on a diet of nectar drawn from night-blooming flowers.

Tree bark is a preferred item in the diet of many mammals. The North American moose consumes it in large quantities, and the bark of willows, poplars and aspens forms the winter diet for beavers of the same region. The North American porcupine lives largely on the inner bark of evergreens and

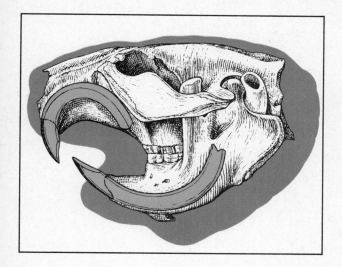

Rodents' Self-sharpening Chisels

The East African mole rat and the naked mole rat show off the incisors they constantly sharpen as they gnaw their way through soil. The cross section of the skull of another rodent, the beaver (*near left*), shows how this self-sharpening works. The incisors (*orange*) grow steadily, with the hard enamel in front backed by soft dentine. As the animal chews, the back is worn away, leaving chisellike teeth.

hardwoods, and its incisor teeth are well adapted for stripping the bark from the trees. In winter, when other food is scarce, rabbits often eat bark taken from the lower trunks and branches of young trees; this causes so much damage to the trees that rabbits are considered a major menace to forestry in some areas.

Fungi, such as mushrooms and lichens, are not eaten very often by herbivorous mammals. Deer and rodents, however, do consume them when they are obtainable, and red squirrels sometimes stick mushrooms on branches to serve as a future food supply. Nuts, on the other hand, are often eaten by many mammals, especially rodents and primates. Squirrels are particularly fond of hazelnuts, which they open by gnawing a hole in the shells with their incisors. Deer, black bears and other species feast on acorns and beechnuts after these

have fallen to the ground during the fall.

Certain species show interesting adaptations to special diets. The kangaroo rats and pocket mice, for instance, of the Southwestern deserts of the United States survive quite well on dry seeds with a water content of less than 10 per cent. Some of these animals may spend their entire lives without ever drinking a single drop of water. On the same diet a brown rat will quickly die of thirst. Obviously the bodies of these desert species are exceptionally well adapted for life on the dry side.

The cud-chewing mammals, or ruminants, have developed another interesting adaptation for digesting food. Many visitors to farms have watched cows placidly chewing, as if on a satisfying brand of gum. The chewing actually is part of the cow's unusual digestive machinery. Like most ruminants,

(*Text continued on page 77*)

Location Fixed by Eating Habits

Mammals are generally found where plant life suits them. This is shown by a study of the Hsifan Mountains of western China, where the climate ranges from subtropical to arctic. At about 3,000 feet the goral, a rock goat, roams the sparse meadows. In the bamboo forests at 6,000 feet lives the giant panda. The lesser panda and orange snub-nosed monkey inhabit the rhododendron thickets at 8,000 feet. Bulky takins spend the summer in evergreen woods at 10,000 feet. Finally, herds of bharal, or blue sheep, graze at 15,000 feet.

Sharp-toothed Veld Grazers

The giant sable antelope, one of the grazing
mammals found on the African veld, has teeth that
are adapted to the tough grasses it feeds on. Through
evolution, this animal has developed strong teeth
with many layers of grinding surfaces; the ridges are
kept sharp by the combined action of the abrasive
silica found in the grass and the rough grains of sand
picked up as the antelope crops close to the ground.

the cow has an exceptionally complicated four-chambered stomach. Food taken into the mouth is chewed for a short time, then swallowed almost whole and passed into the first chamber. Here bacteria begin to work, breaking down the food into simpler, more digestible substances. The food then goes directly to the second chamber where the breaking-down process continues. From the second chamber the pulpy mass is returned to the animal's mouth for more chewing. It is at this stage that the cow is often seen standing very still with a faraway look on its face, chewing and chewing and chewing. After this, the food is passed directly to the third and then the fourth chambers, where chemical action continues to change the food into a form in which it can be absorbed by the body.

Many herbivorous mammals spend much of their time eating or looking for something to eat. For example, a full-grown African elephant may weigh as much as six tons, and it needs between 300 and 400 pounds of fodder each day to keep up its strength. To find this much food requires constant effort; an elephant's waking hours are one long mealtime. Of course, their size makes elephants an extreme example. Nonetheless, it is true that a vegetarian animal spends far more time eating than does a carnivore of a similar size. This is because the plants that the herbivore feeds on offer much less nourishment, pound for pound, than does protein-rich meat.

While the meat eater need not feed all day long, it often has a more difficult time obtaining its occasional meal than the vegetarian has finding enough fodder to graze on.

Among the most efficient of all carnivores are the members of the cat family. Cats of one species or another have spread to almost every region of the world, which shows how successful they have been in adapting to different conditions. Two African cats, the cheetah and the lion, offer good examples of the techniques used by these meat eaters to find food.

The cheetah, found in both Africa and Asia, has a slim, muscular build and exceptionally long legs. The world's fastest land animal, it feeds largely on small, swift-running antelopes and gazelles. When the cheetah spots a herd of grazing gazelles, it moves slowly toward them, carefully approaching from downwind so that the breeze will not carry its scent to the intended victims and warn them off. If a gazelle spots the cheetah, the cat freezes on the spot, becoming less noticeable to its prey. Slowly, very slowly, the cheetah creeps forward. At last it is in range for a quick kill. It springs forward at top speed and leaps upon its quarry before the unlucky gazelle has had time to realize its danger.

The lion, more heavily built than the cheetah, is not so speedy. It relies more on cunning and cooperative effort when hunting its prey—usually zebras or large antelopes such as gnus, hartebeests and elands.

Lions often hunt in couples, the male stampeding the game into the powerful jaws of the waiting female.

All meat-eating mammals normally fear man, but on occasions both lions and tigers —and even some of the smaller cats—have been known to turn man-eater. A successful chance attack on a human might lead a cat to lose its fear of man and also to acquire a taste for his flesh. Very old lions and tigers, no longer quick enough to capture more active animals, are sometimes driven by

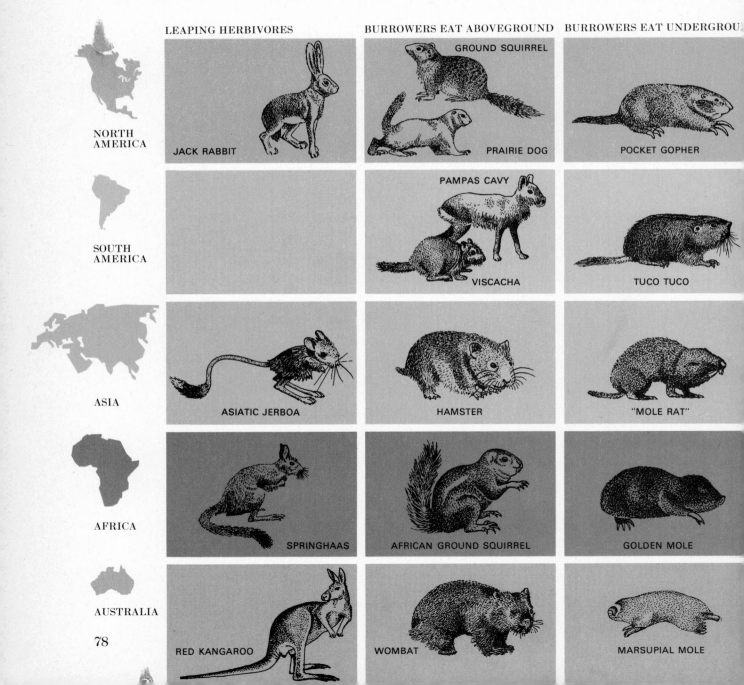

LEAPING HERBIVORES
BURROWERS EAT ABOVEGROUND
BURROWERS EAT UNDERGROU

NORTH AMERICA
JACK RABBIT
GROUND SQUIRREL
PRAIRIE DOG
POCKET GOPHER

SOUTH AMERICA
PAMPAS CAVY
VISCACHA
TUCO TUCO

ASIA
ASIATIC JERBOA
HAMSTER
"MOLE RAT"

AFRICA
SPRINGHAAS
AFRICAN GROUND SQUIRREL
GOLDEN MOLE

AUSTRALIA
RED KANGAROO
WOMBAT
MARSUPIAL MOLE

hunger to become man-eaters. Whatever the cause, man eating among cats seems to run in cycles. This may be because a parent cat, having killed a man, has lost its fear of humans and begins to feed human flesh to its young, giving them an appetite for this meat. Then when the cubs grow up, the whole family of lions or tigers can begin to terrorize a district until they are tracked down and killed by hunters.

After the cats, the weasel and dog families contain the greatest number of meat-

RUNNING HERBIVORES

PRONGHORN

BISON

GUANACO

PAMPAS DEER

SAIGA

WILD HORSE

ZEBRA

SPRINGBOK

RUNNING CARNIVORES

COYOTE

MANED WOLF

PALLAS CAT

CHEETAH

LION

TASMANIAN "WOLF"

Widespread Similarities

All the mammals at left inhabit the world's grasslands. Despite the physical similarities of the animals in each of the vertical columns, none is closely related. They are, however, ecological equivalents—animals of different ancestry that live under similar conditions; they resemble each other because they have adapted successfully to similar surroundings. Thus the vertically grouped mammals, whether they come from the North American plains and prairies, the South American pampas, the Asian t'sao-yüan, the African veld or the Australian savanna, have common traits, including diet and locomotion.

Long Solutions, Short Supplies

The giraffe munching on treetop leaves and the elephant reaching for tender shoots have evolved entirely different solutions to the problem of getting at food. Like the specialized teeth on page 70, the giraffe's long neck and the elephant's long trunk are examples of how an animal's physical shape is linked with its diet. The elephant can also use its trunk to scent food or danger.

eating species. Differing from cats, dogs rely much more on teamwork in hunting their prey. For example, the wild hunting dogs of Africa roam in packs some 20 to 30 strong. The leader of the pack scouts ahead at a distance of several hundred yards. As soon as he sights prey, he takes off full tilt after it. With his great speed, he usually succeeds in getting ahead of the slower members of the game herd. Reversing his course, the lead dog turns the stragglers around and sets them racing directly into the jaws of the dog pack coming up from behind.

As a group, dogs can generally be outrun by cats over a short distance. But dogs tire less quickly, and this superior stamina makes them more than the cat's equal over a long distance. It is this fact that accounts for the dog's direct attack, which may mean running at full speed for hundreds of yards. On the other hand, a member of the cat family, through careful stalking and patient waiting, tries to place itself in a position where its explosive burst of speed will be needed only for the few seconds it takes to seize its prey.

Many mammals are adapted to capturing and eating only particular kinds of prey. The majority of adult seals and sea lions, for example, feast on fish, while their young may be partial to shellfish, such as prawns. The common seal, found in northern waters, consumes between 10 and 12 pounds of fish daily. Other seal species eat octopus and squid, as well as fish. The streamlined, torpedo-shaped bodies of these sea mammals permit them to move swiftly through the water. This is an invaluable ability when it comes to catching their quick-moving aquatic prey.

Generally speaking, seals and sea lions have little to fear from land-dwelling meat eaters. On occasion, though, they are hunted by polar bears. These huge, white, lumbering beasts sometimes stalk the seals across ice floes. A polar bear out for a lunch of seal meat scrunches down against the snow and ice of the floe and blends into this white background. The seal, seeing no immediate danger, settles down for a short nap in the sun. Then with a sudden rush, the bear falls on its prey and gives it a powerful cuff. A blow from a polar bear's paw is usually enough to paralyze or kill the strongest seal. Even if the seal should spot the onrushing bear, it stands little chance of escape. Its flippers make it as clumsy on the surface of the ice as it is agile in the water below.

Occasionally a polar bear will try a variation on the stalking tactic. It waits in ambush at the breathing holes that the seals keep open in the ice. When the seal sticks its head up from the water to take a breath of fresh air, it is greeted with a stunning punch in the nose.

Otters, like seals and sea lions, are great fisheaters, and their bodies are similarly streamlined. They are, however, considerably less fussy about their food. If fish are not available, otters will happily make do

Unusual Utensils

To satisfy their own special food requirements, the honey possums of Australia (*far left*) and the aye-aye of Madagascar (*left*), a lemur, have evolved unique feeding features. The possum uses a pointed tongue for gathering nectar from flowers; tiny bristles on its tongue pick up insects at the same time. The aye-aye has a long middle finger it uses to flip liquids, like egg yolk, into its mouth.

83

with shellfish, small amphibians, reptiles or the young of water birds. One species, the sea otter, has become almost exclusively an ocean dweller, ranging along the Pacific Coast and offshore islands from the Bering Sea to California. The sea otter sleeps on the surface, moored to floating beds of seaweed, and feeds mainly on crabs, sea urchins and mollusks. One of its favorite foods, found in California waters, is the hard-shelled red abalone. Opening shellfish is not much of a problem for a well-prepared sea otter. It clasps a stone to its chest and floats on its back. Then the otter cracks the shells by pounding them forcefully against the stone.

Apart from such strictly water-dwelling species, there are several other mammals that, while not living in the water, forage there for food. The hare-lipped bat of tropical America (*page 88*) skims along just above the surface, with its heavily clawed hind

Ambush in an Amazon Forest

South American bush dogs pursue a striped paca through an Amazon forest. The fast-running paca, a good swimmer, heads toward the water to escape. The dogs have learned to expect this, so in a move that shows the pack's characteristic cooperation, one dog waits along the river bank *(below right)* in ambush.

limbs trailing in the water. These claws scoop up any small fish with which they come in contact. The fishing cat of tropical Asia *(page 89)* is another expert angler. It waits patiently on a riverbank for a fish to swim by, then swiftly dips a forepaw beneath the surface to snag its victim.

One of the most extreme physical adaptations to a particular diet belongs to the various anteater species. The most spectacular member of this group is the giant anteater of South and Central America, which may measure six feet from nose tip to tail. Its nose alone stretches to about 20 inches in length, though it is scarcely an inch wide at the tip.

The anteater's slim, sticky, wormlike tongue reaches out 15 inches from its mouth opening, which is located at the very tip of its long snout. This long tongue sweeps through the chambers of a termite mound. The scurrying termites stick to the surface of the tongue as it sweeps back and forth, and in this way the anteater gathers several thousand of these small creatures to make a single meal.

Several other mammals of different orders have developed a long, sticky tongue for feeding. Among them are the marsupial called the banded anteater and the echidna, a long-snouted monotreme of New Guinea. Neither is a close relative of the true anteater, but they have tubelike snouts and sticky tongues and a similar diet.

One question about mammalian feeding habits that still lacks a complete answer is whether or not animals taste food in the same way humans do. If so, do they sometimes base their preferences purely on flavor? A pet dog will select favorite morsels from its dinner plate before eating the rest. But some zoologists believe that this evidence of choice comes from the dog's long association with man and does not represent its true nature.

In the case of wild animals, there is evidence that elephants, at least, do have food preferences. Around the slopes of Africa's Mount Kenya, for example, there is a large elephant population and also a rich supply of plant food. Yet every January and February the elephants migrate to the higher slopes of the mountain to gorge themselves on the berries ripening there. Since these berries are no more nutritious than the vegetation in the lowlands, it would seem that the elephants make the difficult journey merely to satisfy their taste buds.

Acrobatic Flying Phalangers

Four sugar gliders perch high in the branches of an oak tree, where they sleep during the day and from which they glide down at night for their food. Some members of this Australian phalanger family can sail as far as 120 yards through the air with the aid of kitelike membranes and tails used as rudders.

The elephant's appetite for certain foods has, on occasion, made it seem all too human. An African elephant was once reported to have developed such a strong taste for fermented millet—an alcohol-rich cereal mash—that it made nightly raids on native villages to guzzle the boiled grain. In another instance a whole herd of elephants habitually fed on the fermenting fruit of the umganu tree, which also has a high alcohol content. According to one observer "the elephants, after eating it, became quite tipsy, staggering about . . . screaming so as to be heard miles off and not seldom having tremendous fights."

If the elephant is typical, it is probable that most, if not all, mammals are able to discriminate between the tastes, and effects, of different foods. But this is not yet certain.

While it is doubtful that animals "think" of the future, many mammals—like man—store away extra food for later use. Chipmunks and some deer mice stuff seeds or nuts into their cheek pouches and carry them to their underground storerooms to save them for future needs. Gray squirrels hide nuts in crevices of trees and bury them all over the forest floor; some of these nuts are dug up and eaten later, but many are forgotten and left to take root and grow into new trees.

It is not only rodents that store food. Mammals as different as bears, moles and even leopards are known to store away provisions. The same instinct causes a dog to

Diets with Great Variety

Unlike some mammals that can eat only plants or only meats, the raccoon can make a meal out of almost anything, from persimmons *(top)* or corn *(center)* to fish *(bottom)*. Such easy-to-please eaters are called omnivores, or eaters of all things. The raccoon also feeds on small mammals, birds, reptiles, nuts and seeds. Other omnivores are rats, bears, foxes, skunks, opossums and, of course, men.

A Trio of Fishermen

There is more than one way to catch a fish, as these mammals prove by attacking their prey from the air, water and land. At night the hare-lipped bat rakes the water with its claws, snaring fish near the surface. The otter, a superb swimmer, catches fish in the water but eats its food on dry land. The Asian fishing cat crouches on the bank and scoops up fish with its claws.

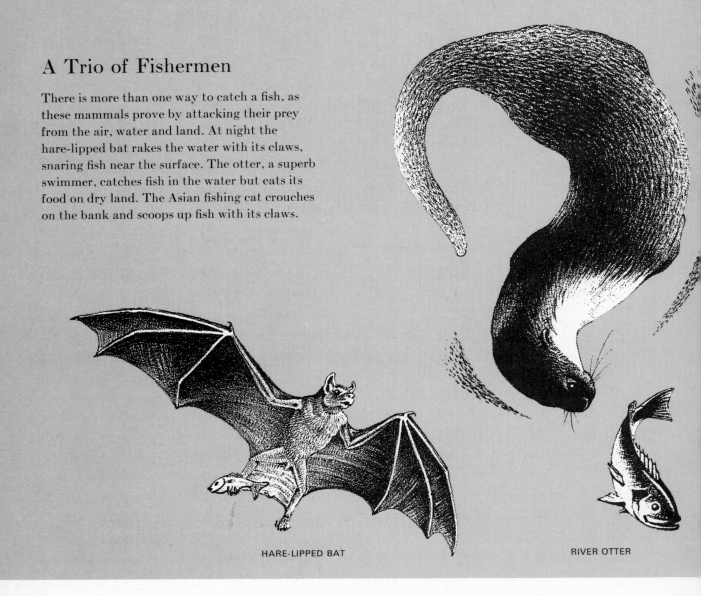

HARE-LIPPED BAT

RIVER OTTER

bury a half-finished bone, the red fox to bury its kill in the snow or under a light covering of dirt and the leopard to divide its victim into portions, some to be eaten immediately, others to be saved for future meals. Among smaller mammals, certain moles are famous for their saving instincts; stocks of a thousand or more earthworms have been found in their burrows. To keep the worms from escaping, the moles bite them near the front of their bodies. This paralyzes the worms but keeps them alive and fresh for future consumption. Moles, incidentally, have truly fantastic appetites. Some have been known to consume their own weight in food every 24 hours.

Another interesting, though little-known fact about some species of mammals is their

88

ability to kill—or at least paralyze—their victims with venom. Almost everybody knows that some snakes and other reptiles have this ability, but such a weapon is hardly ever associated with mammals. In fact, little work has yet been done on this subject, but there is considerable evidence to show that certain shrews produce poisonous secretions similar to snake venom.

In Europe, shrews had long been suspected of being venomous, but the first case of shrew poisoning in North America was not recorded until 1889. In that year there was a fully documented report of a man who had been bitten on the hand by a short-tailed shrew that he had picked up. Within a few seconds he began to experience burning sensations, swelling and shooting pains in his hand and arm. For three days he could not use his hand without feeling great pain.

It was not until 1942, however, that the naturalist O. P. Pearson proved, by experiments with mice, that venom from the glands of the short-tailed shrew caused a lowering of the blood pressure, a slowing of the heart and difficulty in breathing. In small animals, such as mice, shrew venom is capable of producing a state of semi-consciousness in less than a minute. There seems to be little doubt that the species of shrew capable of producing poison from its glands uses this weapon as a highly effective method of paralyzing its victims, which can then be killed and eaten without further struggle.

Are there any lessons to be learned from the eating habits of mammals that will shed light on the evolutionary process? One obvious answer is that the specialized feeding habits and equipment of the various species have helped them survive and prosper. But it must also be remembered that their victory over the challenges posed by nature is never final, for the time may come when changing conditions will make their specialized habits and equipment useless.

What, for example, would happen to the lion and tiger if there was a sudden drop in the number of animals on which they feed? The chances are good that these cats, being totally unfitted for a vegetarian diet, would quickly disappear. And how would the cats' prey survive if the plants that form their diets were to vanish? If changes like these take place—and they frequently occurred during the earth's long history—the only creatures that will survive are those that can successfully adapt themselves to eat different kinds of food.

Certainly the immense success of the brown rat, which today is found in almost every corner of the world, is closely connected with its ability to eat almost anything that comes its way—from wax candles to lizards, from insects and garbage to seeds of plants. And even in the mammal we call man, the same principle applies. It is the enormous adaptability of this species, in diet as in so many other activities, that has been a major factor in man's tremendous achievements.

A Rodent's Refreshment

Daintily dissecting a dandelion, a prairie dog prepares the vegetable part of its diet. These rodents, which live in underground colonies that may spread over several acres, compete with livestock for grass, their main food. But they occasionally feed on grasshoppers to supplement their vegetarian diet.

6

Attack and Defense in the Fight for Life

A BABY TAPIR with a striped coat blends into the foliage of the South American lowland forest, thus giving some protection against attackers. But the stripes disappear as the animal matures, and then its safety depends on its speed and agility in darting into tunnels it has carved out of the dense foliage.

Like all animals, mammals have to struggle to stay alive. Meat eaters like the wolf or tiger must hunt for their food or starve. Most plant-eating animals are caught and eaten if they are not constantly on guard against their enemies. During untold ages of struggle, many mammals have evolved special weapons for attack and defense, without which they might not survive.

The horns of antelope and the antlers of deer are two examples of such weapons. Both are used to ward off attacks as well as to fight other members of the same species. But although they are used for the same purpose and look alike, horns and antlers actually have very different structures. Horns, which are found on such mammals as cattle, sheep and goats, are permanently attached to the skull and keep growing throughout the animal's life. In most species, horns appear on both the males and females. Each horn consists of a bony core jutting out from the skull and covered with keratin, the material of which human fingernails are formed.

The antlers of deer differ from horns because they are shed and regrown each year and consist of bone. Usually only the males

A New Coat for Each Season

The northern weasel changes its coat to fit the season. This molting process is geared to give the protection needed as the seasons change. In March or April, when the snow disappears and bare earth begins to show, dark hairs appear. By May the weasel is brown, except for its belly. In October, another molt begins, this time with white hairs dappling the dark coat; by November, the weasel has its white winter coat.

MAY

APRIL

OCTOBER

NOVEMBER

of a species grow antlers, and they use them mainly in the fights that occur between rival bucks during the mating season. Each spring the bucks' antlers start growing as small bony bumps covered with a delicate, furry skin called velvet. As summer progresses, the bumps enlarge and branch out. Their final size is determined by the age and physical condition of the buck—young animals have only short, straight prongs, while animals in their prime may have elaborate branches. At the beginning of the mating season, the velvet begins to dry up, and the buck rubs it off on tree trunks or branches. This leaves his antlers bare and sharp in preparation for fighting. Although the bucks fight savagely, they seldom kill each other. On rare occasions two will crash together with such force that they lock antlers and eventually they both starve to death. After

95

COMMON GIRAFFE

RETICULATED GIRAFFE

each mating season the antlers drop off and the bucks become docile as the antlers grow out again.

Another weapon that has become highly developed in mammals is teeth. Many mammals, such as the big cats that specialize in offensive attacks, have sharp, daggerlike "eye teeth," or canines. These fangs were extremely well developed in the now-extinct saber-toothed tiger, which probably used its long daggers for stabbing prey. Many mam-

mals that exist today, however, have equally remarkable canines. In walruses, for instance, these teeth have developed into long tusks, which the animal uses for digging up shellfish as well as for fighting. The hides of old walrus bulls are often covered with scars marking wounds inflicted by the tusks of rival males.

An elephant's tusks, too, are derived from teeth, but from the incisors, or front teeth, rather than from the canines. Few animals

THOMSON'S GAZELLE

BUSHBUCK

BURCHELL'S ZEBRA

GREVY'S ZEBRA

Camouflage to Fit the Locale

An animal's protective coloration reflects its living place and means of defense. Plains dwellers have markings that delay recognition by enemies. For example, Thomson's gazelles have confusing black side bands, and the boldly patterned Burchell's zebras look gray at dusk, when lions hunt. The other animals on these pages are forest and bush dwellers whose markings merge with their surroundings. Their white-streaked sides resemble sunlight filtering through foliage; they seem nearly invisible when standing still.

OKAPI

BONGO

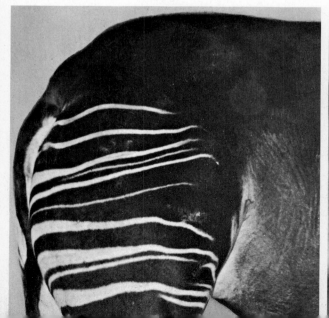

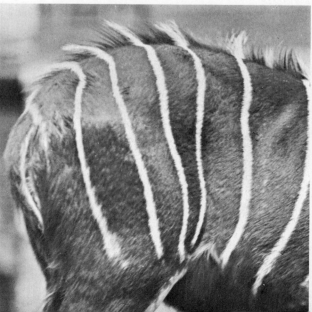

are bold enough to attack a full-grown elephant, but the young calves are tempting prey for big cats, and adult elephants use their tusks to protect their offspring.

Some small mammals have developed an entirely different way of protecting themselves—they have armor. Armadillos, for instance (*page 100*), are covered with thick,

IMPALA

Guidance and Warning Signals

Markings may serve uses other than camouflage. The impala (*left*), which avoids danger by running, has black spots on its heels. During flight from an enemy, these markings help the herd to keep together as it follows the leader. The springbok (*right*) also relies on speed for safety. When excited, it "pronks," or leaps with an arched back. The raised white crest on its back acts as an alarm to others in the herd.

bony plates that make it very difficult for their enemies to get at a vital organ. Some armadillos can even roll themselves up into a tight ball so that it is virtually impossible for even the most persistent predator to get at their soft underbelly. One remarkable armadillo (*page 101*) has a cloak of scales over its back, as well as a thick, bony shield over its tail and hindquarters. When threatened by another animal, the armadillo bolts into its burrow and stops up the entrance with its armored rear.

Spines are another valuable means of self-defense; the prickly surface of a rolled-up hedgehog is enough to discourage most predators. The African porcupine has on its back

SPRINGBOK AT REST   SPRINGBOK PRONKING

Armored Protection

Armadillos belong to an order of mammals that has evolved a scaly hide for defense. When attacked, they protect themselves by curling into a ball or lying flat on the ground. The *Chlamyphorus*, or fairy armadillo, lacks full armor; it ducks into its burrow when endangered, protected by its armored backside.

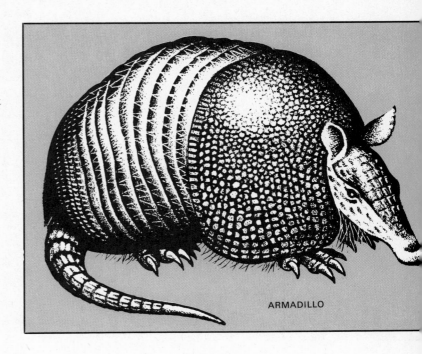

ARMADILLO

an array of quills up to 15 inches long, which can be raised at will. When it is disturbed by an enemy, this animal grunts, snorts a warning, raises the quills and rubs them together to make a threatening sound. If the attacker persists, the porcupine moves backward in a sudden charge. If the quills touch the attacker, they pierce its hide. Even a lion may be killed when these quills penetrate its liver and lungs.

In addition to weapons and armor, many mammals have developed definite color patterns that serve as camouflage to hide them from their predators or their prey (*pages 96 and 97*). The spotted pattern of the leopards, for example, is very effective in concealing them in the woods where they hunt. Similarly, the zebras' stripes and the gi-

raffes' blotches make them practically invisible in thin cover, especially at dusk when they are most likely to be attacked. When we see the bright colors of these animals in a zoo, it is hard to believe that their designs can serve as camouflage. But if we realize that most mammals are color-blind, we can understand how effective the markings are since color-blind animals see only the patterns, which merge with the background.

Color variations are important means of protection. There are instances of closely related members of the same species with variations in color that reflect an evolutionary change to match their surroundings. For example, those pocket mice that live on pale sand dunes in New Mexico are almost white. Members of the same species that live on dark lava flows in the same area are prac-

100

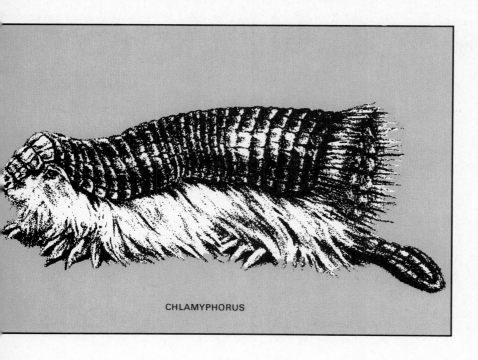

CHLAMYPHORUS

tically black. It is easy to see how these different races developed: the animals that did not match their surroundings must have been easy prey for predators, while those with good camouflage survived and passed on their coloring to their young.

To match their surroundings even more exactly, some mammals actually change the color of their coats at different seasons of the year (*pages 94 and 95*). In the far north certain foxes and hares have a white coat in winter and thus match the snow, but grow a dark coat in the summer to blend in with warm-weather vegetation. A number of forest animals, too, change their color with the season. In summer, when leaves on the trees produce a dappled forest light, the common European fallow deer has a white-spotted coat. But in winter, when the leaves are off the trees and a spotted coat would be conspicuous, the deer grows a uniformly grayish-brown coat.

For some mammals, color serves not as camouflage but as a warning to other animals. Skunks, for instance, have coats with an easily seen black-and-white pattern. It seems clear that these colors act as a warning that says, in effect, "attack me at your peril." When attacked, skunks display their colors aggressively. If this display fails to frighten off the attacker, the skunks spray out a foul-smelling fluid from glands under their tails, aiming the discharge with great precision in the direction of the foe. Once an attacker has been sprayed, it is likely always to remember to give a wide berth to animals with black-and-white markings.

Even mammals with no specially developed weapons or color patterns for defense have ways of protecting themselves. Many have learned patterns of behavior that can help them out of a tight spot. Rabbits or deer, for instance, often "freeze" when they detect an enemy, staying so completely still that they escape detection. The opossum has the ability to play dead when it is attacked. An opossum caught by a dog, for instance, will fall down on its side and draw back its lips in a deathlike grimace. The opossum also has withered-looking ears and a bare tail, so its act is usually convincing enough to make the dog give up and go away after a few sniffs. Once the coast is clear the opossum "comes back to life" and goes about its normal activities.

Of all the many defense mechanisms that mammals have, perhaps none is more amazing than the one developed by several small mice as a last-ditch effort to save their skins. If grabbed by the tail, these mice can actually shed the skin of the tail—but not the bone or muscle—leaving their startled attackers with a small mouthful, but no mouse.

A Herd Sprints for Safety

Galloping in a compact group, pronghorns—the
swiftest of American mammals—stampede across a
Nevada range. A pronghorn, which outruns its
enemies, is equipped for speed. It has sure feet,
enormous windpipe and lungs and a heart twice the
size of that of a sheep of comparable weight.

7

Family Life among the Mammals

From personal experience, everyone is familiar with the family life of human beings, in which children are nourished, taught and protected until they are able to take care of themselves. What may not be so well known is the fact that the family unit is also a valuable training ground for the individual of most other mammal species.

While the family unit is important to every kind of mammal, its make-up differs from one species to the next. In some, such as the bats, the insect eaters and many rodents, the young never know their father, who disappears soon after mating. The children depend instead on their mother for food, shelter and training. In others—the beavers and most primates, for example— the father plays a role of importance.

Some mammalian families last only as long as the young are helpless. Then they

MOTHER LIONS and their young amble along a road in a South African game preserve. Such a group, called a pride, can be composed of one family or of several. The pride hunts as a unit. In addition, it is the school in which the cubs receive the instruction that will turn them into capable adult lions.

105

Courtship Rites

Mammals tend to be more selective than other animals in choosing mates; as part of their courtship, mammals will often fight to get or keep particular companions. Thus, two male elephant seals (*right*) square off to win possession of a group of cows. Strong males will accumulate harems of up to 30 females. The male and female hippopotamus (*below*) are engaged in mid-river, open-mouthed courtship. The male has probably fought off rivals to gain this mate.

break up and the members go off to establish new relationships. For other mammals, the family remains intact for years.

Family life originates with courtship and mating, which takes place for most mammals during the time when the female is fertile—that is, when the female's egg shifts into a position within her body where it can be fertilized by the male's sperm cells. The intervals between periods of fertility vary greatly with different mammals. In many species found in temperate climates, such as deer, the female's egg is in position to receive sperm cells only once a year, in the fall. This makes it certain that the young will be born in the spring, when there is an ample food supply for the nursing mother.

In other species, however, the eggs move into position several times during the year. The female deer mouse, for example, is fertile at eight-week intervals.

After mating, most male rodents, insect eaters and bats leave their partners forever. In other species, such as seals and deer, the males are only slightly more constant in their affections. They seek the company of several females and remain with this "harem" for one mating season. But there are mammals, such as foxes, wolves and many primates (including man) that remain faithful to one female for years.

As soon as a mammalian egg is fertilized, it begins to develop into a baby within the mother. As noted in Chapter 1, however, there are some exceptions to this rule. Mono-

FOOD RESERVE

tremes lay their eggs, which develop outside the mother's body, and marsupials give birth to young at a very early stage of their development.

The period between mating and birth—called gestation—is generally related to the size of the adult animal. Thus, small rodents may be born within three or four weeks of mating, but a zebra infant develops for a year inside its mother's body, a giraffe for 15 months and an elephant for about 21.

Some mammals give birth to litters of a dozen or more infants. Others—including most primates—generally give birth to only one infant at a time.

Primates are unusual, also, in the amount of attention they lavish on their young. Even the primitive lemur shows a remarkable capacity for maternal care. Soon after a lemur infant is born it learns to cling tightly to the fur of its mother's underside. The mother responds by curling her tail be-

The Beaver's Watery Sanctuary

The family life of a beaver centers in its lodge made of branches, stone and mud. The water backed up by a dam serves as an all-weather route to shore. The pool is also a reservoir for plant food. Beavers generally have only one mate. Within each colony, the oldest male is the boss. When his male offspring reach mating age, they are chased out of the lodge and forced to start another colony of their own.

LODGE   DAM

tween her legs to form a cradle on which the infant can lie while still holding tight with all four limbs. From time to time the mother lemur sits upright and bends over her baby to make a low-pitched crooning sound that might be called a lemur lullaby.

With all primates, parental care continues for an exceptionally long time. Man is the outstanding example of this prolonged dependency, for in most civilized societies the child does not become independent of his family until he reaches his teens or early 20s.

The long dependence of young primates reflects the slowness of their physical development. By comparison, young plant-eating animals are well developed at birth. This is understandable, for their survival depends very largely on the ability to escape predators, and agility and speed are the most essential ingredients of survival. The young giraffe, antelope or wild horse can stand

(*Text continued on page 112*)

ve to 15, but may on occasion number 200 bulls, cows and calves.

when it is only a few minutes old and can run quite speedily within a couple of days. But while they are mobile, these animals are not independent, and they require relatively long periods of parental care.

Most meat eaters receive parental guidance for long periods of time. This makes a good deal of sense, for the meat eaters are often born blind and are unable to stand or walk for weeks or months. When they become mobile, they must undergo a complicated learning process if they are to survive. All this education requires a long period of watching and learning from the parents.

Lion cubs, for example, first accompany their parents on hunting forays when they are only a few months old. Standing off at a safe distance, they watch their parents attack and kill the prey, and then they rush in to share the food. After 10 months or so, when their canine teeth are well developed, the cubs begin to hunt their own prey. Even

then the parents stand by, ready to leap to their offspring's aid if necessary.

Very often the mammalian family group forms a unit within a larger organization made up of several closely related families. A herd of cattle or a pride of lions (*pages 104 and 105*) includes a whole range of relations: fathers, mothers, cousins, aunts and uncles. Sometimes these clans are loosely organized, but often each group has an acknowledged leader who takes command of the young and the weak.

In these societies, order of rank is firmly established. Those low on the social scale are required to give way to their superiors. When approached by a superior, a low-ranking wolf, for example, is expected to cringe and make anxious-to-please movements. If it does not, the leader wolf will probably raise its tail and fur, bare its teeth and move threateningly toward the rebel.

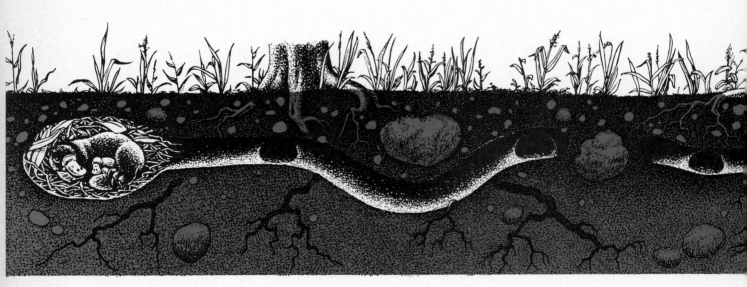

But despite such humiliations, few of the "oppressed" ever leave the clan The idea of safety in numbers is a strong instinct, and for most herd mammals a life alone will be a short one.

There are exceptions, however. It is not rare to find solitary elephants. These animals are so big and powerful that they have little to fear from predators. On the other hand, large groups of 200 or more elephants are sometimes seen. Despite appearances, such large groups do not represent true societies. Rather, these large herds form because many smaller herds, each with its own organization, have come together.

Recently, 450 baboons were found at a water hole. These might easily have been mistaken for members of a single troop. But investigators discovered that there were really three troops present, and the members of each totally ignored the others. As each

Underground Lodgings

The platypus, a native of Australia, lives in a long, winding burrow that opens on a riverbank. At the end of the burrow is a leaf-lined chamber (*left*) in which the female cares for its young. Rooting up the river bottom with its ducklike bill (*below, center*) one adult searches for the small animals on which it feeds; another couple (*below, right*) go through courtship rites, in the course of which they swim in circles, roll over and tweak each other's tails.

troop moved away from the water hole it formed into a definite order of march. This is a common tactic among mammals on the move, and its purpose is to provide maximum protection for the young, the females and the weak. Among the baboons the weaker males lead the way. They are followed closely by females and older children, then by the leader males and nursing mothers. Finally, the remaining adult males bring up the rear. Thus, a predator attacking from any direction will be met with the maximum strength of the organization.

One of the most family-minded of all mammals is the beaver. Beavers create artificial ponds by damming streams with tree trunks. Safe within the moat created by the pond, the animals build lodges constructed of timber and mud (*pages 108 and 109*). The trees for both dam and lodge are felled by the beavers' sharp incisor teeth and are cemented together with stones and earth. The dam keeps the pond deep enough so that the water at the bottom will not freeze in winter.

This permits the beavers to use the underwater entrances to their lodges all year.

In each beaver colony the father is the leader, and he shows considerable aggressiveness toward the males of other colonies and also toward his own sons when they reach breeding age. Young males are driven out and must establish their own colonies when they are two years old. The smaller male youngsters, however, remain in the colony, but both they and their father move out of the main lodge before a new litter is born. For several months they live in temporary quarters nearby—leaving the mother, the female young and the new litter in the main lodge. Most of the work of building the dams and lodges is done by the male beavers, but the females sometimes help when they are not busy bearing and rearing their young.

All mammalian families—from complex man to simple herbivores—have one essential purpose: to ready the young for adulthood—to insure the survival of the species.

A Time for Growth and Care

A mother raccoon grooms one baby as the rest of the litter nurses. This kind of care is a mammalian trait, but the length of protection varies, depending on how much young mammals have to learn to survive as adults. Raccoons shelter their young for up to a year, while mice are on their own in about six weeks.

TREE SHREWS, the most primitive living primates, resemble the mammals that took to the trees millions of years ago to found the primate order, to which man belongs. The lively tree shrews lack some primate characteristics such as grasping hands and sharp vision, but they have skulls with primate traits.

8

Man's Special Place among the Mammals

Man is a mammal. Only 100 years ago, many people were shocked at the idea that man might be related to other creatures. But few people deny it today. A trip to the monkey house at the zoo provides numerous examples of the outward similarity between men, apes and monkeys: the way a chimpanzee grimaces, or an orangutan uses its nimble fingers to break open an orange, or a mother gorilla carries her baby—all these are startlingly similar to human behavior.

Further evidence of man's relationship to the primates comes from the science of comparative anatomy—the study of how bones, muscles and internal organs are arranged in different animals. Scientists have discovered, for instance, that the human skeleton contains exactly the same number and kind of bones as the gorilla or chimpanzee. And even in less advanced primates, in which the number of bones differs, their arrangement is very similar. Still more evidence of man's ties to other primates is found in the structure of the front legs and arms, which in all but the most primitive primates are extremely well adapted to grasping. Perhaps the most significant evidence of kinship comes from the

Evolutionary Steppingstone

The tree-dwelling *Notharctus*, which disappeared ages ago, moved through trees with the aid of offset fingers. This animal was one of the first primates to have a "thumb" clearly set apart from its other toes, a feature that enabled it to grasp. Fossils of the animal some 58 million years old show that *Notharctus* was an evolutionary step between tree shrews and monkeys.

structure of the human brain, which is identical in its basic plan to that of an ape. In fact, human intelligence is superior to that of apes, not because man has special brain parts, but because he has succeeded in developing parts of the brain that all primates share.

Although the fact that man is a mammal is most obvious when he is compared with other primates, it is also proved by his likeness to certain other mammals. As we have already seen, such characteristics as warm-bloodedness and milk glands for feeding the young are possessed by man and all other mammals and are clear evidence of kinship. Moreover, when the limbs of mammals as different as the horse, the sea lion and the bat are examined, it becomes evident that all are made up of basically the same combination

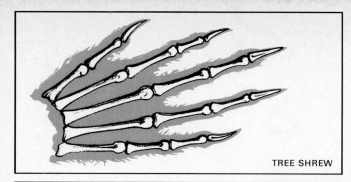

TREE SHREW

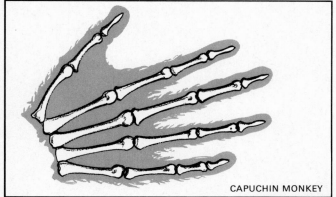

CAPUCHIN MONKEY

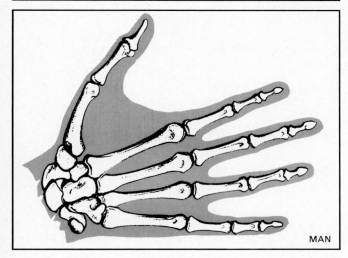

MAN

The Key to a Flexible Hand

The most primitive primates lack an opposable thumb—the useful finger that can press from the opposite direction against the other four, enabling hands to grasp or pick up objects. The tree shrew has limited grasping abilities. The monkey, however, has a thumb set at an angle so it can encircle and hold objects. Man, too, has a large, opposable thumb, giving him a versatile hand.

of bones that make up human arms and legs.

Despite his similarities to other animals, man has a special place among mammals. One of the best ways to understand this is to study his evolutionary history.

The steps by which man has evolved from lower primates are now fairly clear, although some gaps still remain in the record. The story started in the Age of Reptiles, some 180

million years ago, when the first mammals were scurrying to keep out of the way of giant reptiles like dinosaurs. As the Age of Mammals dawned, a group of primates including tree shrews, tarsiers and lemurs had taken up residence in the treetops, a way of life that seemed to increase their chances of survival.

To live successfully in the swaying tree-

A Larger Use of Eyes

The heads of these South American night monkeys show several important primate features. The large eyes face forward to help them judge the distance between objects. Improved vision goes hand in hand with a lessened dependence on smell, as indicated by flattened noses. Finally, rounded skulls point to a greater brain capacity and a sharp intelligence.

tops, these animals had developed a variety of structural changes that were to have immense significance in the evolution of man. Their fingers and toes were longer to aid in holding onto branches. The front and hind limbs were specialized for different functions: the front legs were more flexible and better suited for reaching upward, and the more muscular hind legs supported the animal's weight while it was climbing. Most important, the highly developed parts of the brain that enable a creature to touch what it sees helped the animals move efficiently through swaying branches.

The special significance of these adaptations to the development of man came when one group of primates, which included man's ancestors, was forced to move back to the ground. This move was necessary because a changing climate had reduced forest areas. When these primates climbed down from their tree homes, their muscular hind limbs, used for climbing, were adapted into strong supporting legs that allowed the animals to walk upright. This freed their already flexible arms for the vitally important jobs of making weapons and tools. Meanwhile, the changes that had occurred in the brain during life in the trees were well suited to the development of intelligence and quick-wittedness.

The exact stages by which man's ancestors evolved throughout the Age of Mammals cannot be traced with great precision, because primate fossils are much less common than those of other mammals. This is partly because, even when they have become mainly ground dwellers, primates normally live in or near forested areas, and conditions in these areas are not ideal for the preservation of bones in fossil form. Another reason is that these intelligent and active creatures seldom drown, and one of the main ways in which the remains of animals come to be preserved in rocks is through being encased in the muddy bottoms of rivers and lakes.

Nevertheless, scientists have found several interesting fossils that belong to advanced apes very close to the human line of descent. These include two creatures known as *Dryopithecus* (the tree ape), whose remains have been found in the Siwalik Hills of India, and another, found in the Victoria Nyanza region of East Africa, called *Proconsul* (named after "Consul," a famous chimpanzee that once lived in the London Zoo). Although neither is in the direct ancestral line to man, both certainly have an excellent claim to be regarded as very close relations of man. Fossils have also been found of other creatures, much later in time than the two just mentioned, which are even more manlike; of special interest are *Australopithecus*, the "southern ape" of Africa, *Pithecanthropus*, the "man-ape" of Asia, and still later, Neanderthal man, a true man of Europe and the Middle East.

In terms of geological time, man's development was extremely swift—he reached his present stage in about two million years. In some ways, in fact, that time has been too short for man's body to adjust to its new way of life. The two-legged stance, for instance, puts a terrible strain on his back and his abdomen. As a result, many humans suffer from backaches; many others have hernias, for gravity's pull causes the intestines to burst through the abdominal wall.

In spite of physical imperfections, man has triumphed over his fellow mammals, most of whom seem to have better natural physical equipment. An unarmed man, for instance, would be no match for the lethal claws and teeth of a tiger. His puny canine teeth are completely ineffective as weapons. Yet they are very important to his survival. Because they are not specially adapted for eating one particular kind of food, as is the

case with strictly meat-eating or plant-eating mammals, man's teeth allow him to eat a variety of foods; he is not handicapped by having to depend on just one of them. And his brain makes up for the fact that he has lost his natural weapons. Superior reasoning powers led even our most primitive human ancestors to use spears, darts, and clubs to

The Primate Brain at Work

As it frolics from one branch to another, an orangutan makes constant use of its brain. This specialized primate brain allows the animal to make full use of advantages such as its opposable thumb, its more acute vision and its greater ability to learn by remembering the lessons of past experiences.

fend off attacks and to kill their quarry. Similarly, though man is a very inferior runner compared to many mammals, he has built machines that carry him faster than the fastest mammal can run.

In fact, many of the specialized physical advantages with which other mammals are born have been reinvented by man to serve his own purposes. Knives and daggers, for example, do the work that canine teeth did for the predatory animals. The metal armor that soldiers used in medieval times, for instance, was joined in just the same way that an armadillo's natural armor is, to allow movement and still give protection. There is one area in particular in which man shows a tremendous advance over any other mammal, and that is in the organization of his society. Many mammals cooperate with one another—wolves hunt in packs, lions live in families and many grazing animals group together for defense. But in all of these groups all the animals perform roughly the same job; there are few specialized tasks that can be done by only some members of the group. In human societies, however, specialization is the rule, and it leads to greater efficiency. To get an idea of the difference between the lives of people and those of other animals, try to imagine what it would be like if everyone had to grow his own food, make his own clothes, heal his sick relatives, manufacture his own car and build his own house.

As you can see, there are many differences between man and other mammals. But the question remains: what single thing is it that makes the human species unique? The answer is probably man's ability to think abstractly, that is, to think about the future or about things he can't see. A chimpanzee, for instance, is thinking when he uses a stick to reach for a banana, but he is not thinking abstractly the way a caveman did when he chipped an arrowhead out of a piece of stone for use in a future hunt. The chimpanzee is merely solving a pressing problem without thinking about general methods of reaching bananas. The caveman could think about an imaginary hunt and then make a tool that would serve him in any hunting situation. This ability to think in abstract terms is a most important requirement not only for toolmaking, but for speech, for writing and for the understanding that has led to scientific, artistic and philosophical thought. His highly developed ability sets man apart from his fellow mammals and makes him human.

A New Kind of Evolution

Sprawled in lazy repose, a young orangutan displays
a very human look of wonderment. The ability of
primates—including man—to show emotions stems
from their complex brains. However, even this brain,
like the cheetah's speed and the elephant's strength,
is only an adaptation useful for survival.

Index

Numerals in italics indicate a photograph
or painting of the subject listed.

For Further Reading

Adamson, Joy, *Born Free: A Lioness of Two Worlds.* Pantheon, 1960.

Andrews, Roy Chapman, *All about Whales.* Random House, 1954.

Blond, Georges, *The Great Migrations.* Macmillan, 1956.

Bronson, Wilfred S., *Horns and Antlers.* Harcourt, 1945.

Buck, Margaret Waring, *In Woods and Fields.* Abingdon, 1950.

Cosgrove, Margaret, *The Strange World of Animal Senses.* Dodd, 1961.

Darling, Louis, *Kangaroos and Other Animals with Pockets.* Morrow, 1958.

Gidal, Sonia and Tim, *Follow the Reindeer.* Pantheon, 1959.

Green, Ivah, *Wildlife in Danger.* Coward, 1959.

Hyde, Margaret O., *Animal Clocks and Compasses.* Whittlesey, 1960.

Lauber, Patricia, *The Friendly Dolphins.* Random House, 1963.

Ley, Willy, *Exotic Zoology.* Viking, 1959.

Lorenz, Konrad Z., *King Solomon's Ring.* Crowell, 1952.

Mason, George F.:
Animal Habits. Morrow, 1959.
Animal Sounds. Morrow, 1948.

Animal Tails. Morrow, 1958.
Animal Teeth. Morrow, 1965.
Animal Tracks. Morrow, 1943.
Wildlife of North America. Ed. by J. P. Colby. Hastings, 1966.

Mellin, Jeanne, *Horses across the Ages.* Dutton, 1954.

National Geographic Society, *Wild Animals of North America.* National Geographic Society, 1960.

Reidman, Sarah R. and Elton T. Gustafson, *Home Is the Sea: For Whales.* Rand McNally, 1966.

Ripper, Charles L.:
Bats. Morrow, 1954.

Moles and Shrews. Morrow, 1957.

Rounds, Glen:
Swamp Life: An Almanac. Prentice-Hall, 1957.
Wildlife at Your Doorstep. Prentice-Hall, 1958.

Scheele, William E.:
First Mammals. World, 1955.
Prehistoric Man and the Primates. World Publishers, 1957.

Williamson, Margaret, *First Book of Mammals.* Watts, 1957.

Zim, Herbert S.:
Great Whales. Morrow, 1951.
Mice, Men and Elephants. Harcourt, 1942.

Credits

The sources for the illustrations that appear in this book are shown below. Credits for the pictures from left to right are separated by commas, from top to bottom by dashes.

Cover—Oscar Schmid from Photo Researchers Inc.
Table of contents—Rudolf Freund—Joseph Cellini—Eva Cellini—Mark A. Binn—Guy Tudor—Lowell Hess—Lowell Hess—Lowell Hess
6—Nina Leen
8—Rudolf Freund except lower right Betty Davis
10, 11—René Martin
12—René Martin
13—Left Lowell Hess, right Leslie Martin
15—Andreas Feininger
16, 17—Rudolf Freund
23—Andreas Feininger
24—Rudolf Freund
26, 27—Joseph Cellini
28, 29—Rudolf Freund
30, 31—Joseph Cellini
32, 33—Joseph Cellini
35—Howard Sochurek
36—Robert W. Kelley
37—Fritz Goro
38, 39—Rudolf Freund

41—Jean B. Thorpe
42—John Dominis
44, 45—Ralph Morse (Kangaroo Victoria courtesy Animal Talent Scouts New York City)
46, 47—Ylla from Rapho Guillumette
48, 49—Eva Cellini
50, 51—Otto van Eersel
52—Lewis W. Walker, Arizona Sonora Desert Museum
55—Andreas Feininger
56, 57—Fritz Goro
58, 59—Maps by Adolph E. Brotman and animals by Mark A. Binn
60, 61—George Silk
62, 63—Otto van Eersel
64, 65—Matt Greene
66, 67—H. V. Vuori
68—Fritz Goro
70—Hans Zillessen
72—Jack J. Kunz
73—Leslie Martin
74, 75—Joseph Cellini
76—Grass by Margaret L.

Estey and animal by Joseph Cellini
78, 79—Matt Greene
80—Baron Hans von Meiss-Teuffen from Photo Researchers, Inc.
81—Commander Gatti from Free Lance Photographers Guild
82—Guy Tudor
83—Jack J. Kunz
84, 85—Rudolf Freund
86—John Dominis
87—Karl Maslowski from Photo Researchers, Inc.—Andreas Feininger—Leonard Lee Rue III from Annan Photo Features
88, 89—Rudolf Freund
91—Wallace Kirkland
92—Francis Miller
94, 95—Rudolf Freund
96—George Holton of Photo Researchers, Inc., Des Barlett—Armand Denis of Photo Researchers, Inc.—

N. Meyers of Free Lance Photographers Guild, Jane Burton of Photo Researchers, Inc.
97—Top Paul Jensen—Robert Cohen from AGIP New York Zoological Photo
98, 99—Jack J. Kunz
100—Lowell Hess
101—Eva Cellini
102, 103—George Silk
104, 105—Satour
106, 107—George Silk—Pete Turner from Free Lance Photographers Guild
108, 109—Lowell Hess
110, 111—Eliot Elisofon
112, 113—Margaret E. Estey
115—W. Vandivert
116—Nina Leen
118—Lowell Hess
119—Louis and Lois Darling
120—Dmitri Kessel
122, 123—Michael Rougier
125—Michael Rougier
End papers—Virginia Wells

Acknowledgments

The editors of this book are indebted to Richard Van Gelder, Chairman, Department of Mammalogy, The American Museum of Natural History, New York City, who read the entire text. The editors are also indebted to the staff of the LIFE Nature Library from which this volume has been adapted. The staff for this edition was Stanley Fillmore, editor; Eric Gluckman, designer; Peter Chaitin, Marianna Kastner, Victor Waldrop, writers; Eleanor Feltser, Tony Chiu, Susan Marcus, Theo Pascal, researchers; Eleanore W. Karsten, copyreader; Virginia Wells, art assistant.